TAPS

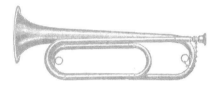

ALSO BY RICHARD SCHNEIDER

Freedom's Holy Light

Why Christmas Trees Aren't Perfect

TAPS

NOTES FROM A
NATION'S HEART

Richard H. Schneider

wm

WILLIAM MORROW
An Imprint of HarperCollins*Publishers*

Pages 133–134 serve as an extension of this copyright page.

HarperCollins books may be purchased for educational, business,
or sales promotional use. For information please write: Special Markets
Department, HarperCollins Publishers, Inc., 10 East 53rd Street,
New York, NY 10022.

FIRST EDITION

Designed by Betty Lew

Printed on acid-free paper

Library of Congress Cataloging-in-Publication Data has been applied for.

ISBN 0-06-009693-4

02 03 04 05 06 ❖/RRD 10 9 8 7 6 5 4 3 2 1

To Betty,

THE GIRL WHO SOUNDED THE ECHO . . .

AND LATER BECAME MY WIFE

Contents

CONTENTS

vii

One of the most precious gifts—maybe the single most precious gift—our fathers bestowed upon us, when they returned home from World War II, was a world so much quieter and more peaceful than the one in which they had lived on the battlefields of Europe and the Pacific. It was as if they wanted us, their sons and daughters, not to give a thought to what they had spent their young manhoods enduring.

And so we grew up with that illusion—the illusion they had won for us, the illusion they wanted us to believe, the illusion that nothing could go wrong. But we knew—on some level we knew how much more difficult their lives had been than ours. We would be in bed at night at some pleasant and carefree summer camp, surrounded by other children in their own bunks in a happy facsimile of an Army barracks, and from somewhere on the campgrounds would come the last sound of the evening, that trumpet sound like no other.

We knew. It was the final sound, every night—and no one had to explain. It was a sound from our fathers' lives, their good night to us. "Day is done . . . "

—Bob Greene, author of
Once Upon a Town and *Duty*

In December 2001, I had the privilege of participating in two ceremonies commemorating the sixtieth anniversary of the Japanese attacks on Pearl Harbor and Hickam Airfield.

During each of these ceremonies I could not help but be moved by the sight of the storied veterans of those attacks. As the bugle sounded the first note of "Taps," these men crisply rose to attention. Despite their hands being gnarled with the passage of time, they saluted smartly, tears slowly running down their cheeks.

Scenes such as this have been replayed time and again across our great land. No other tune has such haunting power and none can so movingly bring to mind the sacrifices of those brave men and women who have served their country.

In the wake of the tragic events of September 11, 2001, no other melody focuses the mind so clearly on the price of freedom. "Taps" reminds us that despite the tragic costs, it is worth defending.

—Richard B. Myers, General,
United States Air Force

A U.S. soldier plays "Taps" on Omaha Beach during the D day invasion.

Solace

He'll never forget it. His first night in a drafty Army barracks. A frightened, bewildered kid away from home for the first time, in shock after a horrendous day. His head shorn, his lanky frame stuffed in an ill-fitting, scratchy wool uniform, a drill sergeant screaming at him in language not heard at home.

He lay rigid, trembling, wondering what tomorrow would bring. Then it sounded. Distant, melodious bugle notes wafting through the night. "Taps." He had heard them before, in Scout camp and elsewhere. He even remembered some of the words.

> *Day is done, gone the sun . . .*
> *All is well, safely rest*
> *God is nigh . . .*

So familiar, so comforting; he relaxed and was soon asleep.

I was that first-night soldier during World War II. And that memory of "Taps" comes to mind each time I hear its hauntingly beautiful melody at funerals, wreath layings, and Memo-

For a soldier, "Taps" is both the most welcome and the most feared sound. When I was a young lieutenant in training at Fort Benning, it was the most welcome sound, as it signaled the end of the soldier's long day. Later, in Vietnam, this was doubly true, as our days were often spent in combat.

But at other times, of course, hearing "Taps" was not so welcome, as it meant a fellow soldier had fallen. We were reminded that there, but for the grace of God, go I.

—*Senator Max Cleland*
(Dem., Ga.), Vietnam veteran

rial Day ceremonies. Its poignancy especially moved me as I heard it played so often in commemoration of those who died in the terrorist attacks on September 11, 2001.

I had assumed that "Taps" had been around forever and was part of every nation's tradition. But not until a year ago did I learn its interesting—and distinctly American—story.

"Taps" was born during one of the most tragic conflicts in our nation's history, the Civil War. A romantic myth about how it began is so widely circulated that many people believe it to be fact.

The real story of "Taps," told in the following pages, begins in a spirit of deep compassion during one of the darkest nights of the war. From its creation, "Taps" flew throughout our nation on the wings of intense human emotion to become the indelible twenty-four notes in our nation's music that it is today. It is a song with a soul to which every heart responds. During its 140 years with us, it has accumulated its own lore and legends, which are recounted in this book. "Taps" continues to resonate in American hearts, here and around the world, to this day.

U.S. Army corporal Richard Schneider, Belgium, 1944.

As Oliver Willcox Norton, the bugler who first played "Taps," wrote years later: "There is something singularly beautiful and appropriate in the music of this wonderful call. Its strains are melancholy, yet full of rest and peace. Its echoes linger in the heart long after its tones have ceased to vibrate in the air."

They linger in my heart today, long after that first night when I needed them most.

I pray that you, too, will be blessed by the comfort they were meant to give.

—Richard H. Schneider,
Rye, New York, January 2002

Introduction: Solace

To me, "Taps" are the most beautiful notes ever produced. My memory of "Taps" begins in 1950 when I was seven and was spending the summer at camp in Maine. At night, lying there in the deep woods, the lights would go out at ten, then someone played "Taps" on the camp bugle. Those notes wafted slowly into the night air, echoed across the quiet lake, answered only by the loons far out on the lake. A quiet peace would settle over the five hundred young and restless campers.

As a Marine Corps Vietnam veteran, I am now more moved than ever by the notes of "Taps." At every veteran's funeral, every Memorial Day service, "Taps" signals our special moment of saying, "Thank you for your duty to our country and to the citizens and their freedom."

"Taps" always brings me to a quiet, peaceful place in my heart. I am at once sad and happy. Sad that I lost so many young friends in the war, and happy that I knew them and their courage.

—*Bob Spear,*
Marine Corps Vietnam veteran

CHAPTER ONE

"Butterfield's Lullaby"

*I*t was a terrible time to be a soldier that hot July night in 1862 at Harrison's Landing in southern Virginia.

The 140,000 exhausted, demoralized Union men encamped in soggy mud along the James River sweated in the heavy humidity and the stench of offal and open latrines. They cursed as they slapped at the ravenous mosquitoes and biting flies that were torturing them. Their sunken eyes stared dully at flickering campfires. Many sodden blue uniforms bore stains of blood, feces, and mucus brought on by bouts with dysentery. Men delirious with fever tore off heavy woolen shirts to reveal skin blotched with the rose-colored spots of typhoid. Soldiers died daily, their bodies wrapped in gray blankets and hastily buried along the riverbank.

Only three months earlier, these men of the Army of the Potomac under General George McClellan had confidently boarded ships near Washington, D.C., expecting to end the Civil War by capturing the Confederate capital of Richmond. The Southern rebellion would then be over, less than a year after it started.

McClellan's strategy had been to sail down Chesapeake Bay to Virginia's Lower Peninsula between the York and James Rivers and march the sixty miles up to victory in Richmond.

Though his troops reached the suburbs of Richmond, Confederate forces repulsed them. Furious fighting culminated in the famed Seven Days Battles, waged June 26 to July 1 between McClellan and General Robert E. Lee. The carnage was horrible. A Union colonel, on viewing a slope where five thousand Confederate soldiers had fallen, wrote: "Our ears had been filled with agonizing cries from thousands before the fog was lifted, but now our eyes saw five thousand dead or wounded men on the ground. A third of them were dead or dying, but enough of them were alive and moving to give the battlefield a singular crawling effect."

Lee's forces suffered twenty thousand casualties; McClellan's, sixteen thousand.

The Confederate leader fell back to Richmond to rest his troops. The ever-cautious McClellan withdrew south, down to Harrison's Landing at Berkeley Plantation on the James River, where Union gunboats provided relative safety.

Despite two visits by an anxious President Abraham Lincoln trying to prod McClellan into advancing on Richmond, the reluctant general stayed put. Poor intelligence reports had led him to believe he faced superior Confederate forces. In reality, the Reb soldiers in Richmond were in a sorry state; had McClellan attacked at this point, he probably could have taken the city.

Meanwhile, heavy rain turned mud into soup. When the downpour finally stopped, a searing July sun emerged, ripen-

President Lincoln twice visited General McClellan and his federal army at Berkeley Plantation in 1862, the year in which "Taps" was written.

ing the fetid atmosphere and causing millions of flies and mosquitoes to hatch and fresh water to be in short supply.

Severely wounded and dying men were quartered in Berkeley Plantation's three-story Georgian manor house crowning the hill. Then 136 years old, the gracious redbrick mansion overlooking the broad James had already achieved its own place in history.

Built by Colonel Benjamin Harrison IV, the mansion had been passed down to his son Benjamin, a signer of the Declaration of Independence and three-time governor of Virginia. The colonel's third son, William Henry Harrison, born at

Berkeley, became the famous fighter "Tippecanoe," and the ninth president of the United States. Forty-seven years later his grandson, another Benjamin Harrison, would become America's twenty-third president.

Some of Berkeley Plantation's "firsts" include the claim that it was the site of America's first official Thanksgiving, celebrated on December 4, 1619, by English settlers who came ashore there. The plantation is also where the first bourbon whiskey was distilled in America (1621–1622).

One of the Union officers most likely to have appreciated Berkeley's history was Brigadier General Daniel Adams Butterfield, commander of the Third Brigade of the Fifth Army Corps, Army of the Potomac, a scholarly thirty-one-year-old former law student from Utica, New York.

Instead of being ensconced in the luxurious home that had hosted George Washington and nine succeeding presidents, Butterfield camped in a tent close to his men. It was a typical canvas officer's shelter, oppressively hot during the day and dank at night. The only concession to Butterfield's rank was a bower of leafy branches that stretched over his and neighboring headquarters tents. From within his tent, the scratching of the general's pen could be heard late into the night as he sat at his portable desk, writing reports praising the valor of his soldiers.

Butterfield had a deep compassion for his men and had risked his own life many times to ensure their safety. On June 27, during a particularly critical moment during the Seven Days battles at Gaines Mill and while still recovering from a serious wound received in battle the week before, Butterfield seized the falling colors of his Third Pennsylvania Regiment to rally his troops and charge the enemy lines. This act of bravery, which helped Union forces to safely withdraw to Harrison's Landing, earned him the Congressional Medal of Honor.

It's easy to picture Butterfield, on that hot night in early July, wincing from his wound as he hoisted himself from an army cot and stepped outside his tent. As he stood looking over the campfires flickering in the darkness, his heart must have been heavy. So many of

"Bugle Call": Civil War bugler calls an advance in the midst of battle.

his young men had been lost in the recent battles. So many were grievously wounded or diseased. Now the pitiful remnants were forced to endure miserable squalor. Who could go to sleep peacefully under such wretched conditions? And sleep is what the soldiers so sorely needed.

Butterfield pulled out his watch. It would soon be time for his bugler to signal "extinguish lights." He had never really liked this call; to him it was colorless and harsh, not at all soothing.

He looked again at his men; voices drifted up in a low disconsolate mutter. A deep compassion filled him.

"Tattoo & Reveille": the two most important bugle calls in a soldier's day.

He turned and asked his orderly to summon the brigade bugler.

Shortly, twenty-three-year-old Private Oliver Willcox Norton appeared carrying his bugle. He must have wondered why he was being called to headquarters. "O.W.," as his friends and family called him, had enlisted in Pennsylvania when the war broke out and eventually became part of the Eighty-third Pennsylvania Volunteers under the command of the man whom he now saluted.

The general sat in a camp chair outside his tent. An oil lamp cast an amber glow. Butterfield returned Norton's salute and told him he felt the men needed something more comforting than the standard bugle call.

As Norton wrote later:

General Daniel Butterfield . . . showing me some notes on a staff written in pencil on the back of an envelope, asked me to sound them on my bugle. I did this several times, playing the music as written. He changed it somewhat, lengthening some notes and shortening others, but retaining the melody as he first gave it to me. After getting it to his satisfaction, he directed me to sound that call for "Taps" thereafter in place of the regulation call. The music was beautiful on that still summer night, and was heard far beyond the limits of our brigade. The next day I was visited by several buglers from neighboring brigades, asking for copies of the music, which I gladly furnished. I think no general order was issued from army headquarters authorizing the substitution of this for the regulation call, but as each brigade commander exercised his own discretion in such minor matters, the call was gradually taken up through the Army of the Potomac. I have been told that it was carried to the Western Armies by the 11th and 12th Corps, when they went to Chattanooga in the fall of 1863, and rapidly made its way through those armies.

As word of the new "Taps" spread throughout the Union forces, it also came to be known by another name: "Butterfield's Lullaby."

Evidence of the moving effect of the new call is seen in its first recorded use at a military funeral. Though McClellan's troops saw relatively little ground combat at Harrison's Landing, they did exchange shell fire with the Confederates. Artillery emplacements, along with Union gunboats on the James, offered good targets. Battery A of the Union's Second

This painting by Sidney King depicts General Daniel Butterfield and his bugler, Oliver W. Norton, working out the notes to "Taps." (Note that the drummer boy on the left is John Jamieson, who returned to Berkeley Plantation more than fifty years later to purchase and renovate it.)

Artillery fired from an advanced position in the woods. (Another source says it was B Battery of the Third Artillery.) During a fiery exchange, a Confederate shell exploded near the Union battery, killing a cannoneer.

The Bugler at Chickamauga Creek

Chickamauga is an old Cherokee word for "river of death." The Chickamauga Creek is therefore appropriately named, for it was the site of one of the bloodiest battles of the Civil War.

The Confederate Army of Tennessee and the Union Army of the Cumberland collided in a titanic clash on September 19, 1863, near Chickamauga Creek, eight miles south of Chattanooga. The Union forces were routed that first day of what turned out to be a two-month struggle, and they fell back to Chattanooga. Both sides suffered many thousands killed and wounded.

It would have been worse for the Union Army that September day if it hadn't been for Bugler William J. Carson, Company E, First Battalion, Fifteenth U.S. Infantry. At a critical moment, when the Fourteenth Corps lines were in disarray, Carson, on his own initiative, sounded a rousing "To the colors!" The nearby Eighteenth U.S. Infantry rallied around him and held off the enemy. Then, amid the smoke and shell fire, Carson noticed the second Ohio Infantry wavering. Dashing over, he again blew his inspiring call. Hearing the bugling, Confederate forces thought reinforcements had arrived and held off on their attack, thereby saving many Union soldiers. Two months later Union troops launched a powerful counterattack and achieved a stunning victory.

For his bravery and initiative, William Carson was awarded the Congressional Medal of Honor, our country's highest military decoration.

When the time came to bury the slain soldier, the battery captain, John C. Tidball, was faced with a dilemma. Traditionally, three rifle volleys were fired over the grave at the funeral. Surveying the nearby enemy lines, Tidball worried. Would hearing rifle fire so close make the Confederates think Union infantry was advancing and cause them to renew the fighting? What could he do? He looked at his rifle squad, muskets ready.

Then he remembered the haunting new call that had so recently been sounded by General Butterfield's bugler. That was it, he decided. What better way to send a departed comrade off to his final sleep?

And so the rifles were slung, a bugler was called, and the strains of "Taps" sounded over the grave of a soldier for the first time in history.

This practice caught on throughout the Army of the Potomac and eventually became a tradition at all military funerals. An early reference to its official use can be found in the *U.S. Army Infantry Drill Regulations* for 1891.

As the soothing tones of "Taps" drifted across Harrison's Landing, it is very likely that Confederate forces heard and liked it. Rebel soldiers lurked in the underbrush across the James River, and J. E. B. Stuart's gray-cloaked cavalry con-

> "Taps" was familiar to me even before entering the service. It became even more important to me during World War II. And now, after September 11, I take special comfort in its message: "All is well, safely rest, God is nigh."
>
> —*Archie Marconi,*
> *World War II veteran*

stantly patrolled outside the encampment. One report tells of "Taps" being played at Confederate General Stonewall Jackson's funeral ten months later. In fact, the Confederate Army's *Mounted Artillery Drill* manual published in 1863, states: "Taps will be blown at nine o'clock, at which time all officers and enlisted men must be in quarters." Ironically, the new call could well have been the first unguent in healing the wounds suffered by the bitterly opposing sides.

Meanwhile, as the fighting at Harrison's Landing dwindled to some sporadic shelling and skirmishes between the opposing forces, it became apparent to the high command in Washington, D.C., that the grand campaign to take Richmond was a lost cause. The Civil War would go on for another three years.

The Army of the Potomac began its withdrawal north on August 15, some soldiers by Navy ship, others by wagon train. All that remained was the heritage of "Taps," notes that bring comfort to listeners today as they first did for those dispirited and suffering soldiers in the mud at Harrison's Landing.

> When I hear the lonesome sound of "Taps" I have mixed emotions. I get a feeling of sadness thinking about the men and women who gave their lives for their country, but also pride and a feeling of security knowing people are fighting for our liberty and freedom. God bless them.
>
> —*Randy Travis,*
> *actor and musician*

CHAPTER TWO

The Myths

From Elvis spottings in Manitowoc, Wisconsin, to spaceships crashing in Roswell, New Mexico, urban legends seem to have a life of their own, especially when it comes to national icons . . . and "Taps" is certainly no exception.

TATTERED NOTES IN A POCKET

When I first started to explore the history of "Taps," the following account was presented to me as the true story of the creation and composition of the famous tune. It's truly a remarkably compelling story, full of pathos and drama.

> We have all heard the haunting song, "Taps." It's the song that gives us that lump in our throats and usually creates tears in our eyes.
>
> But, do you know the story behind the song? If not, I think you will be pleased to find out about its humble beginnings.

Reportedly, it all began in 1862 during the Civil War, when Union army captain Robert Ellicombe was with his men near Harrison's Landing in Virginia. The Confederate army was on the other side of the narrow strip of land. During the night, Captain Ellicombe heard the moans of a soldier who lay severely wounded on the field. Not knowing if it was a Union or Confederate soldier, the captain decided to risk his life and bring the stricken man back for medical attention.

Crawling on his stomach through the gunfire, the captain reached the stricken soldier and began pulling him toward his encampment. When the captain finally reached his own lines, he discovered it was actually a Confederate soldier, but the soldier was dead. The captain lit a lantern and suddenly caught his breath and went numb with shock. In the dim light, he saw the face of the soldier.

It was his own son. The boy had been studying music in the South when the war broke out. Without telling his father, the boy enlisted in the Confederate army. The following morning, heartbroken, the father asked permission of his superiors to give his son a full military burial despite his enemy status. His request was only partially granted. The captain had asked if he could have a group of army band members play a funeral dirge for his son at the funeral. The request was turned down since the soldier was a Confederate.

But, out of respect for the father, they did say they could give him only one musician. The captain chose a bugler. He asked the bugler to play a series of musical notes he had found on a piece of paper in the pocket of the dead youth's uniform. This wish was granted. The haunting melody, we now know as "Taps" used at military funerals, was born.

A wonderful and heartrending story, right? There's just one problem . . . it's a complete fabrication. A careful check has been made of its facts. There are no military records proving the existence of a Captain Robert Ellicombe (or Ellison, as is sometimes reported). Nor does the narrative mention the captain's unit or state, details that generally accompany a military account. Further research uncovered the true story of General Butterfield and his bugler, as related in chapter I.

The Ellicombe urban legend's first appearance dates back at least seventy years. It

The official dress uniform for buglers of the U.S. Cavalry.

was featured in a "Ripley's Believe It or Not" newspaper cartoon back in the 1930s. Reportedly, it later appeared in a "Dear Abby" column (though to be fair, Abby later ran a retraction once the truth of Butterfield's role came to light). It has appeared in various military magazines through the years under various bylines and has been published in the *Encyclopedia of Amazing but True Facts*. And of course the advent of the Internet, that furious percolator of so many urban legends, has only spurred the dissemination of this sad but untrue story.

THE OTHER BUTTERFIELD

Another interesting legend about "Taps" concerns one Milton Butterfield, a Confederate soldier who enlisted in the Alabama Twenty-third Infantry. As the story goes, he eventually became a captain and served in the defense of Vicksburg during a long siege by Union forces, before the city finally fell in July 1863.

After the war was over, he told a family member about events that happened after a particularly fierce battle. He and his men were finishing up the burial of one soldier who had been a favorite of the troops. Some of the men felt that the occasion called for something a bit more than the standard simple battlefield funeral service. Milton, who happened to be a bugler, was asked if he would play something on his "horn." And so, he recounted, he composed a few simple notes for the burial service, which ultimately became "Taps." Later, while serving in Chickamauga near Chattanooga, Tennessee, he heard that a relative, General Daniel Butterfield, was stationed nearby with the Union forces. While visiting the general under a flag of truce, he told him about the "burial music" he had composed. At the general's request, Milton scribbled the simple notes on an envelope and gave it to Daniel Butterfield.

The trouble with this story is that the dates supplied for it occur long after the actual birth of the call in July of 1862 at Harrison's Landing. The fall of Vicksburg, where cousin Milton supposedly wrote the tune, took place a year later, long after both Union and Confederate troops had started to use the call as their own.

DID BUTTERFIELD PLAGIARIZE "TAPS"?

While not really a myth, there are some scholars who maintain that it is a mistake to fully credit Daniel Butterfield with the actual composition of "Taps." These critics point out that the tune of "Taps" is closely reminiscent of the last five and a quarter bars of what was known as the "Scott Tattoo," a bugle call included in many drill manuals published well before the Civil War began. The strange fact is that Butterfield himself never categorically claimed credit for the actual writing of the song. Here's the story.

In 1898, *The Century Magazine* published an article entitled "The Trumpet in Camp and Battle." In this article, Gustav Kobbé, a noted music historian, discussed the origins of some of the bugle calls used in the U.S. Army, including "Taps." Kobbé stated that he was unable to trace the origins of "the most beautiful of all trumpet-calls."

I had been a Boy Scout bugler, playing "Taps" at every Memorial Day service. My dream was to one day be an Army bugler. By the time I entered the Army in 1964, however, recordings of bugle calls had taken the place of actual buglers. But when I left for Vietnam in 1965 as part of the first combat infantry troops to be sent, I smuggled my old Boy Scout bugle aboard the troopship.

While in-country, our first sergeant allowed me to play "Reveille" and "To the Colors." However, he never allowed me to play "Taps" because, he said, the enemy knew that bugle call and he didn't want to give them the satisfaction of knowing that they had killed some of our troops. Then one day in March of 1966, only a few weeks before our yearlong tour of duty was up, we were caught in an ambush. We really took a beating—I was hit twice by a mine and rifle grenade. I crawled back to my best friend, Ted, and found that he had taken a bullet in the gut. I cradled him in my arms. After calling out for his mother, he died.

After being discharged from the hospital, I was determined to properly honor Ted. My chance came when I learned that a memorial service was going to be held at our base camp for those members of our company recently killed in action. I persuaded the first sergeant to relax his rule this one time and allow me to play "Taps." As I stood with the mouthpiece of my old bugle pressed against my lips, visions of Montgomery Clift playing "Taps" for his dead friend in the movie *From Here to Eternity* passed through my mind. I had made it halfway through "Taps" when tears began to stream down my face. Try as I might, I just couldn't finish. So I stood at attention and saluted the M-14 rifles with their bayonets stuck into the ground and covered with steel helmets, hoping that Ted and the others wouldn't mind. Just then a gentle breeze began to blow and I knew Ted was near and that he understood.

—*Lee Banicki, Vietnam veteran, Charlie Company,*
First Battalion, Eighteenth Infantry

It turns out that one of the readers of *The Century Magazine* was Oliver Willcox Norton, the bugler who assisted Butterfield at the first playing of the call. Norton immediately wrote to *Century*, saying:

> General Daniel Butterfield, then commanding our Brigade, sent for me, and showing me some notes on a staff written in pencil on the back of an envelope, asked me to sound them on my bugle. I did this several times. He changed it somewhat, lengthening some notes and shortening others, but retaining the melody as he first gave it to me. I did not presume to question General Butterfield at the time, but from the manner in which the call was given to me, I have no doubt he composed it in his tent at Harrison's Landing.

Sensing a controversy brewing, the editors at *Century* then asked Butterfield himself to respond. By this time the general was retired and living in Cold Spring, New York—although he was only sixty-seven, he was weary and infirm, his death only two years away at the time he sent this note to *Century*:

> I recall, in dim memory, the substantial truth of the statement made by Norton about bugle calls. His letter gives the impression that I personally wrote the notes for the call. The [bugle] call did not seem to be as smooth, melodious and musical as it should be,

and I called in someone who could write music, and practiced a change in the call until I had it to suit my ear, and then, as Norton writes, got it to my taste without being able to write music or knowing the technical name of any note, but, simply by ear, arranged it.

As you can see, Butterfield does not specifically claim that he wrote the actual notes for "Taps," though neither does he state that he simply revised a previously known call. Norton, of course, did maintain that Butterfield was solely responsible for the composition. Despite the claims of naysayers that Butterfield ought not to be given the credit for this beautiful piece of music, the fact is that Daniel Butterfield was the one who arranged the notes for "Taps," with the assistance of Oliver Norton. Therefore, it seems pointless to dispute the fact that "Butterfield's Lullaby" originated with Butterfield himself. (Another interesting technical note: "Taps" was composed on an Army bugle, an instrument that has a limited number of notes, and just whole notes, at that. Further, there are only three notes used in "Taps": E, C, and G. As Paulette Jiles, author of *Enemy Women,* a novel set during the Civil War, says, "The wonder of it is that such a beautiful melody was composed out of such a limited repertoire of notes.")

As with all wars, the Civil War spawned a number of myths. A few of the more colorful are:

THE GETTYSBURG VULTURES

The Battle of Gettysburg, which took place July 1–3, 1863, resulted in the deaths of fifty-one thousand men and untold numbers of horses and mules. To this day it still remains the bloodiest incident to take place in the United States. One of the most horrible aspects of the aftermath was the army of vultures that descended upon the battlefield, still littered with unburied corpses. For weeks, thousands of vultures fed on both Union and Confederate dead under the oppressive rays of the summer sun. According to one particularly gruesome legend, each year, on the anniversary of the battle, the *same* group of vultures returns to the site of the Gettysburg battle, hoping to discover the results of yet another bloody conflict.

Unfortunately, at least for the believers of this story, a vulture has an average life span of just thirty years, so either the Gettysburg buzzards have found some Carrion Fountain of Youth or they've passed the story on to their young ones. Believe it or not, however, there are some vultures that do frequent the site of the great battle . . . but naturalists assure us that it's because the now-peaceful area offers sheltered roosting sites and plentiful food.

THE WOMAN WHO ADVISED THE PRESIDENT

There's at least one kernel of truth in this particular legend: Anna Ella Carroll of Maryland *did* exist. We've all known people like Ms. Carroll . . . shameless name-droppers who insist

This photograph of dead Confederate soldiers awaiting burial was taken by Alexander Gardner, assistant to famed Civil War photographer Matthew Brady.

on imposing their opinions on anybody and everybody who will listen . . . and even on those who won't.

On January 10, 1862, during some of the bloodiest fighting of the Civil War, Anna Ella Carroll supposedly wrote a letter to the war department outlining a plan she had devised for the Union army to use the Tennessee River as a pathway leading to an invasion of the heartland of the Confederacy. According to the legend, upon receiving the letter, Lincoln immediately recognized its merit and ordered his top generals to follow Anna's plan as written. The campaign that followed resulted in the Union's eventual conquest of the Mississippi Valley.

In June of that year, Anna Carroll wrote again to Abraham Lincoln. In this letter she offered no clever military tactics; instead, she demanded "a substantial and liberal reward" for the Tennessee River plan she had supplied him with in January. Unfortunately for Ms. Carroll, however, the Tennessee River Campaign had been planned for many months before her initial letter was written . . . after all, massive military campaigns are not conceived and executed within a matter of days. Moreover, no record existed of anyone in the government receiving such a letter, much less the president.

An anonymous suffragette playing a bugle. Though Anna Ella Carroll's claim against the federal government for a reward eventually failed, she went on to become a major figure in the women's suffragette movement. (History does not record, however, that she played the bugle!)

Of course, Anna Carroll did not receive her "liberal reward," though one can't fault her for a lack of persistence. She pursued her claim against the government for decades, long after the Civil War was over. In 1890, she actually brought a suit against Congress, though the suit was later dismissed.

Though she never received a penny as a result of her vociferous claims, she did benefit in one respect: she became a cause célèbre for the burgeoning women's suffrage movement.

THE MIRACULOUS MINIÉ-BALL CONCEPTION

Perhaps the most fascinating Civil War myth concerns a miraculous battlefield conception. This story has appeared again and again ever since it ran in *The American Medical Weekly* of November 7, 1874, under the byline of a Confederate field surgeon, LeGrand G. Capers Jr.

> I remember many nights in the Marine Corps, particularly at officers' training in Quantico. I came in from the field, dog tired, with two inches of dirt and mud caked on me. That was grueling stuff, as any Marine officer will remember.
>
> I barely had time at night to get my rifle cleaned and my gear stowed before lights out. I can remember listening to "Taps" being played, beautiful sounds that engulfed the base. In every barracks, hundreds of men at the same time heard that beautiful, calming music.... It's still music that I can rarely hear without feeling goose bumps.
>
> —*Charles Colson, columnist and author; founder of Prison Fellowship Ministries*

During General Grant's advance on Vicksburg, a fierce battle raged most of the day on May 13, 1863, in Raymond, Mississippi. Around three o'clock in the afternoon, Dr. Capers reported seeing a woman and her two teenage daughters imprudently standing in their yard watching the battle. Suddenly a nearby Confederate soldier fell wounded. At the same moment Dr. Capers heard one of the younger women scream.

The minié ball, designed by Captain Claude Etienne Minié of the French army in 1848, became one of the deadliest weapons in the Civil War. It was the first bullet designed with a hollow base, thereby doubling its accurate range on the battlefield.

He attended first to the soldier, whose left leg had been pierced by a Yankee bullet. The bullet—known as a minié ball—had glanced off the bone and traveled up through the leg, destroying the young man's left testicle in its passage. As the doctor finished his work on the soldier, the mother ran up, screaming that one of her daughters had been wounded. Dr. Capers then rushed over to the girl. His examination revealed a bullet hole in her abdomen, and he cleaned and dressed the wound.

Six months later Dr. Capers returned to the town of Raymond. Calling on the farmhouse where he had rendered his services earlier that year, he found the young girl in excellent health—and very pregnant. When the doctor asked her about the baby's father, however, she insisted that she was a virgin and had never been with a man. Familiar with protestations similar to these, Dr. Capers simply smiled and continued with his examination.

Three months later, exactly nine months after the May battle, Dr. Capers helped the young woman deliver a healthy eight-pound baby boy. A few weeks later, however, Capers was called back to examine the baby, who appeared to have a deformation in his genitals. Capers later wrote that he found "an enlarged swollen sensitive scrotum containing on the right side a hard, roughened substance, evidently foreign."

He operated on the infant's testicles and removed a damaged minié ball.

His inference was obvious—this same minié ball had, only ten months earlier, torn through the young Confederate soldier's leg and testicle and traveled on to lodge into the young woman's uterus through the wound in her abdomen. The bullet had picked up sperm from the trip through the scrotum and caused what seemed to be a virginal conception. "There can be no other solution of the phenomenon," Capers told the family.

The storybook ending? The wounded young soldier and the young mother soon married.

At the time of its publication in 1874, this wonderful story was considered to be the unvarnished truth. However, no one was ever able to locate the elusive Dr. Capers. In this story's myriad permutations over the years, Dr. Capers has changed from a Confederate surgeon to a Union surgeon and back again; also, the scene of the battle has varied over the years from Mississippi to Virginia to Georgia.

From a song-pilfering relative to undying vultures, the Maryland matron and presidential adviser to the amazing minié-ball conception—each of these myths adds romance and mystery to Civil War lore. My favorite legend remains, however, that of Captain Robert Ellicombe and his dead son's authorship of "Taps"—a story that, unlike most urban legends, has remained unchanged, almost word for word, over the years.

Growing up on Air Force bases around the world there were certain rituals observed both in our family and as part of the "base family." While stationed at Clark Air Force Base in the Philippines, "Taps" was an especially prominent part of our daily life. During the Vietnam War my father would fly missions from the P.I. to Vietnam. At the end of every day, at 5:00 P.M., "Taps" would sound. First came a siren, then, piped through speakers around the huge expanse of the base, we would hear the short and familiar sound of the bugle. Wherever one was, whatever one was doing, you stopped and assumed a position of respect. Only later, after the POWs were released and came through Clark on their way back to the States, did many of us kids understand the gravity of war, as evidenced by those who did not return.

As a wife, mother, and, most of all, a citizen of the United States, I now have a maturity and understanding of what "Taps" represents and a comprehension of the sacrifice that so many have made. The symbol of that sacrifice for many is wrapped up in twenty-four notes.

—*Cheryl Smith, granddaughter, daughter,*
and wife of career military officers

CHAPTER THREE

The General and the Private

*T*he general and the private who came up with the dramatic new bugle call were unusual men in their own right. Both went on to notable accomplishments in military service and civilian life.

THE COMPASSIONATE GENERAL

Daniel Adams Butterfield came by his leadership skills naturally. His father, John Butterfield, started out as a sharp-witted stagecoach driver in Albany, New York, in the early 1800s. Recognizing the need for fast and efficient long-distance delivery of merchandise, he developed a large network of express stagecoach lines. (I recently saw one of these coaches, emblazoned with the name Butterfield, in an exhibit.)

In 1850, he merged his firm with several other delivery companies to form the American Express Company (now synonymous, of course, with credit cards rather than delivery). Eight years later, before the advent of transcontinental rail service, Butterfield launched America's first overland express service. His Overland Stage Company's U.S. Mail coaches thundered across the plains and through mountain passes from St. Louis to the West Coast in a then-amazing three weeks' time. After these numerous business accomplishments, he turned his attention to politics and successfully ran for mayor of his hometown of Utica, New York.

Daniel Butterfield, John's third son and one of nine siblings, was born in Utica on October 31, 1831. A student leader at Union College in Schenectady, New York, he graduated at age eighteen and went on to study law. Because he was too young to take the bar exam, his adventurous spirit led him to take off on his own, and he journeyed through the West with a Native American guide. While passing through the South on his way to New Orleans, he was appalled at the widespread slavery trade. He returned home soon thereafter, deeply troubled by what he had witnessed, and convinced that the Southern states' institution of slavery made war between the North and the South inevitable.

Back in Utica, he joined the local militia and went to work for his father, preparing a timetable and schedule for the Overland Stage line between Memphis and San Francisco. A few years later he moved to New York City as Eastern superintendent for American Express and became a colonel in the New York State Militia. When the Civil War broke out in April 1861, Butterfield's Twelfth Regiment was assigned guard duty in Washington, D.C., a city already in danger of Confederate attack.

Promoted to brigadier general of the Third Brigade of the Fifth Army Corps, Army of the Potomac, Butterfield distinguished himself in the Battle of Hanover Court House in the

Peninsular Campaign in May 1862. After the battle, his admiring officers presented him with a set of gold spurs.

While on active duty, the indefatigable officer wrote an infantry manual on camp and outpost duty, which was published by Harper & Brothers in 1863.

After the Battle at Gaines Mill on June 27, 1862, Butterfield was awarded the Congressional Medal of Honor for rallying his regiment at a critical moment, thus helping the Army of the Potomac to safely withdraw to Harrison's

General Daniel Butterfield is generally acknowledged to be the arranger of "Taps."

Landing. It was here that Butterfield worked with his bugler to devise the bugle call "Taps."

Military life is regimented, and bugle calls are used to signal the numerous activities that make up a soldier's day. Butterfield, who was a fair bugler himself, had already composed several other calls, including a signal for troops to advance, to halt, to lie prone, and to charge.

At that time (as now), there were many dozens of bugle calls, each one denoting a particular activity or battle action. The soldiers enjoyed composing their own (often bawdy or irreverent) lyrics, such as these words devised for "Reveille":

The General and the Private

I was ten years old when Brigadier General James W. Totten died of cancer in early March 1967. As Uncle Jimmy's godson, I was asked by his wife to lay a wreath in the garden behind their New England farmhouse where his ashes would be interred. It was the first funeral I'd ever attended, and my anxiety at having to bring up the greenery and place it at graveside without stumbling or cracking a self-conscious smile jangled my nerves.

The winter snow had melted, but spring remained hidden beneath the brown remnants of last year's blooms. The mourners were family and friends, and we huddled against the chill in gloves and overcoats. Uncle Jimmy's widow, Ruth Ellen, wore black, and I overheard her chiding herself for crying. She had always joked that all Pattons weep at the drop of a hat, none more so than her late father, my grandfather George S. Patton Jr., who at fraught moments had been as quick to tears as to profanity.

When the moment came to present the wreath, I botched it—or so I thought, for I'd nervously set it atop the urn rather than beside it. Of course no one even noticed, but throughout the rest of the funeral I was so filled with shame that I forgot the day's larger purpose of burying a good man with honor and reverence. Then I heard the bugler begin to play "Taps." Played at sunset on a military post, "Taps" offers a quiet requiem for the day just passed. Played at a military funeral, its scope opens outward, like the bell of the trumpet, from the quotidian to the eternal.

The trumpeter stood somewhere in the woods beyond the garden. His music filtered through the bare trees as if born out of nature itself. A second trumpeter took up the tune from farther in the woods, and then a third a moment later. The result was a layered warble of three lone instruments playing "Taps" in a continuous round, pulling deep sighs from the mourners.

Later I saw three Boy Scouts trudging out of the woods with bugles in hand. I wondered if they'd been nervous about performing at such an occasion and if they truly understood their music's powerful effect. I don't know who arranged for them to play "Taps" that day in 1967, but the music influenced even a skittish ten-year-old like myself to contemplate Jim Totten's life and death with appropriate sorrow and pride.

—Robert H. Patton, grandson of General George S. Patton Jr.; novelist and author of The Pattons: A Personal History of an American Family

"I can't wake 'em up, I can't wake 'em up, I can't wake 'em up in the morning." Butterfield's personal brigade call consisted of three long notes in one key, followed by a repeated catch (similar to a catch in one's voice). To this his men would sing: "Dan, Dan, Dan Butterfield, Butterfield," though one soldier noted wryly that during some rough times he heard "Damn, Damn, Damn, Butterfield."

After the Peninsular Campaign, Butterfield's new call was sounded in many major battles, including Bull Run, Antietam, and Fredericksburg. Butterfield advanced in rank to major general and then became chief of staff of the Army of the Potomac under Generals Hooker and Meade.

His talent for organization came to the fore when General Hooker asked him to develop a system of shoulder patches to identify the many different corps. The need for these patches was illustrated when General Philip Kearny found himself making the embarrassing mistake of dressing down officers who were from another unit.

Butterfield's badges proved popular with the troops. As he wrote later, he designed them "for no reason other than to have some pleasing form of shape, easily and quickly distinguished from others, and capable of aiding in the 'esprit de corps' and elevation of the morale and discipline of the army."

About a year after receiving his first battlefield wound at Gaines Mill, Butterfield was again severely wounded by cannon fire on July 3, 1863, at the Battle of Gettysburg.

Butterfield recovered from his wounds and, after the war, served as the head of the Army's recruiting service in New York City. Always interested in music, he recommended that the Army adopt a new fife-and-drum manual. In 1870, he resigned from the Army to serve in the U.S. Treasury Department under President Ulysses S. Grant. A few years later he rejoined the American Express Company, which had kept him on full salary throughout the war.

Always working, Butterfield continued to perform many civic duties, such as overseeing the funeral of General Sherman in 1891, constructing a railroad in Guatemala, and serving as president of the National Bank in Cold Spring, New York, where he lived on his family's estate, Cragside.

His first wife, whom he married in 1857, died in 1877. Nine years later, at the age of fifty-five, he married Julia Lorillard James of New York City.

Many well-known personages and foreign notables visited the couple at Cragside. It's easy to picture them and their guests sitting on the veranda in the evening as the soft strains of "Taps" drifted across the Hudson River from West Point Military Academy.

On July 17, 1901, Butterfield died at the age of sixtynine. He was buried at West Point with full military honors—and, of course, a lone bugler sounded "Taps" at the end of his funeral service. As a matter of rule, no one who has not attended the Academy may be buried on the grounds, but a special order of the secretary of war made this possible in Butterfield's case, in view of his outstanding service to his country.

The huge and ornate memorial to Butterfield at West Point features sixteen columns engraved with the details of the thirty-eight

The elaborate monument to the memory of Major General Daniel Butterfield (1831–1901) is in West Point Cemetery, West Point, New York.

battles and skirmishes in which he fought. Another monument dedicated to him stands in New York City, near the tomb of his old friend Ulysses S. Grant.

Oddly enough, none of these monuments mentions his

Over the course of my Navy career I have heard the strains of "Taps" played on literally hundreds of occasions. Each time the melody raises a lump in my throat as I reflect on its significance.

On Tuesday, the eleventh of December, the men and women of the Naval Academy paused in a brief ceremony to reflect on the losses suffered by the Academy and our nation during the attacks on America three months prior. As is often the case in commemorations of this nature, a lone bugler played "Taps" at the end of the ceremony. I'm sure it comes as no surprise that there was not a dry eye in the house.

—*John R. Ryan, Vice Admiral, U.S. Navy; superintendent, United States Naval Academy, Annapolis, Maryland*

role in the creation of "Taps." But each time that haunting call is played, it serves as a memorial to the compassionate man who composed it.

THE BUGLER WHO BECAME A MOGUL

The life of Oliver Willcox Norton is another fascinating story of ambition and idealism. Norton was born December 17, 1839, the oldest of thirteen children. His father, a Presbyterian minister, moved his large family many times in the ensuing years.

In 1861, the twenty-two-year-old Norton had become a schoolteacher in Pennsylvania, and supplemented his meager income with day work on a local farm. When news of the Confederate attack on Fort Sumter reached his town, however, Norton raced to the enlistment office and joined the Eighty-third Pennsylvania Volunteers as a bugler under the command of General Daniel Butterfield.

During the war, no matter how rough the times or fierce the battle, Norton regularly wrote lengthy letters to his sister Elizabeth Lane Norton, a "conductor" on the Underground Railroad in Sherman, New York. These letters, more than 150 of them, were later collected into a book titled *Army Letters,* and have proven an invaluable account of the day-to-day life of a soldier in the Civil War.

One of Norton's letters, dated October 9, 1861, reveals the tedium of army life for soldiers not engaged in battle: "The first thing in the morning is drill, then drill, then drill again. Then drill, drill, a little more drill. Then drill, and last, drill. Between drills, we drill and sometimes stop to eat a little and have a roll-call."

Although less than enthusiastic about drilling, Norton was clearly proud of his commander, Butterfield. He wrote to his sister: "I send you a *Harper's* [pictorial magazine], thinking you do not often see them. You see a

Oliver Willcox Norton, the bugler who helped Daniel Butterfield arrange "Taps," went on to become one of the founders of the American Can Company.

good portrait of our 'Little Dan,' too. If I ever get home I'll show you the bugle he took from my hand to 'sound the charge' at Bull Run. I'm proud to see him now Chief of Hooker's staff."

After the momentous battle at Gaines Mill and the composing of "Taps," Butterfield left to become the Army chief of staff. Norton continued to serve under Colonel Strong Vincent, third commander of the Eighty-third Pennsylvania Regiment. Close in age, the two men took to each other from the start. Colonel Vincent had been a Harvard-educated lawyer in Erie, Pennsylvania, before he had enlisted, like Norton, in the patriotic fever following the war's outbreak. Vincent made O.W. his chief bugler and color bearer.

The two fought together in the Battle of Gettysburg where they were caught in fierce action at Little Round Top. In danger of being overrun by heavy Confederate forces, the Eighty-third Pennsylvania Regiment fought back with spirit and vigor and managed to hold their position. But Colonel Vincent was mortally wounded.

"There is no one to fill his place," lamented O.W. to his sister. "No one could march a brigade as he could. Oh, how we loved him!" In later years Norton named his youngest son after Vincent.

In 1863, Norton wrote to his sister: "You know that, with my restless disposition, I could not be content as brigade bugler while there was a possibility of doing better. As long ago as May, I began to work for a commission in a colored regiment."

This was a fearsome—and courageous—step for the young man. African-American troops had been a force in the Union army since the war's commencement. The Confederate soldiers were especially vengeful toward these troops, believing their very existence would cause the Southern slaves to rise up and revolt. Anyone serving in a black regiment could be sure that, if captured, he would suffer a prolonged, agonizing death rather than be sent to a POW camp.

Despite these dangers, O.W. sought such an assignment, and in 1863, he was commissioned as a first lieutenant and served as a regimental quartermaster for the Eighth U.S. Colored Regiment, which battled fiercely in the Battle of Olustee.

In November of 1865, O.W. was honorably discharged and immediately made good use of the business experience he had gained as quartermaster. He got a job with the Fourth National Bank in New York City, where he met and married Lucy Coit Fanning.

After five children had been born, Norton decided to take a bold step and move his family to Chicago to go into business with his brother Edwin, dealing in canning and sheet metal goods. Over the years the business prospered and expanded, and the brothers took on additional partners and clients. In 1901, the Nortons merged their company with a few smaller firms and formed the American Can Company.

> I probably first heard "Taps" when I was in the Navy, in boot training in 1943. You always heard that bugle when the flag was lowered. In a few months I was sent overseas for duty on a rocket boat off Normandy—D day. Hearing it afterward was heartbreaking.
>
> —*Baseball legend Yogi Berra*

But Norton never forgot his days in the military. He was a member of the Grand Army of the Republic (a Civil War service organization much like today's American Legion) and commander of the Illinois chapter of the Military Order of the Loyal Legion.

He also wrote three books about his military service, one of which, *The Attack and Defense of Little Round Top,* is considered by many historians to be the definitive account of that critical and bloody battle.

Norton returned to Little Round Top in 1880 to dedicate its regimental monument and take part in the annual reunion of the battle's survivors. He later reported that, while standing on the rocks of Little Round Top, he sounded the old Dan Butterfield call with his battered wartime bugle. "When the bugle sounded," he wrote, "a great shout came up from the men. . . . They came charging up to the spot where I stood, some with tears in their eyes, asking to have it repeated.

"That familiar sound echoing among the rocks where they had fought," he continued, "brought back, perhaps more vividly than words could do, the memories of the days when they had answered so often to its sound."

In later years Norton built a summer home in Chautauqua, New York, and helped in the construction and funding of the Minerva Free Library in Sherman, New York, the hometown of his sister Elizabeth. The library has established

> I've attended many military funerals and "Taps" is the one part of the service that never changes. It has always been a time for me to silently pay my last respects to a departed comrade and to thank him for his service to our country.
>
> God bless America.
>
> —Bob Dole

a special collection for the entire set of letters that Norton had written home during the long and dangerous days of the War Between the States.

Norton remained close friends with Elizabeth Vincent, the widow of his former commander Colonel Strong Vincent. Upon her death, Norton found that she had left him the sum of $250 to be spent on fine cigars, one of his few indulgences. Rather than send this money up in smoke, Norton contributed the entire amount to an African-American church, perhaps in remembrance of his wartime service with the black troops.

Norton and his old commander Daniel Butterfield did not stay in touch after the war, but years later, in 1898, they were brought back into indirect contact through the editors of *The Century Magazine* upon the publication of the article discussed in chapter 2.

In 1920, at the age of eighty-one, Oliver Willcox Norton died at home in Chicago. His wife, Lucy, donated a sizable portion of his estate to fund the building of an opera house in Chautauqua, New York, the site of their summer home. Remembering her husband's many complaints about the difficulty of following operatic story lines, his widow included a provision in the donation that the hall perform only operas written or translated into English.

The general and the private—Daniel Butterfield and Oliver Willcox Norton—two men who will be forever united in the composition of the world's most moving twenty-four notes.

CHAPTER FOUR

Plastic Bugles and "Dee Den Tap Toe"

I couldn't believe my eyes when, during World War II, I saw a man lift an olive-drab bugle to his lips to sound a call. Was it painted that way for camouflage? Later that evening, when the soldier handed it to me, I was astonished. It was made of *plastic*. To my mind, it seemed to be nothing more than a child's toy. I soon learned that henceforth all Army bugles were to be made of the drab "plastic"—actually a compound known as tenite, an Eastman Kodak product originally used for safety film, hairpins, and doorknobs.

"Why switch to plastic?" I asked.

"It weighs only half as much as a regular bugle and it saves two pounds of brass," said the bugler. "It needs no warming up, so it won't stick to your lips in cold weather. Also, it's almost unbreakable—it doesn't dent, and it'll withstand extreme temperatures. Besides," he added with a smile, "I don't have to polish it."

And to tell the truth, his call sounded fine to me. I later

learned that the plastic bugle had undergone a battery of tests by a cornet soloist of the United States Army Band in Washington, D.C. The Army Band found the plastic bugle superior in tone and equal in volume to the regular brass instruments. (In fact, the bugle in this book's frontispiece photograph, played on Omaha Beach on D day, was made of tenite.)

And yet the plastic bugle never caught on, according to veteran military buglers I talked with recently.

"Taps" being played at the Memorial Day services in New Caledonia in honor of the fallen dead of U.S. Armed Forces, May 30, 1943.

Sounding "Taps" at Ceremonies

As a trumpeter, you may be asked to sound "Taps" at a funeral, memorial service, or wreath-laying ceremony. The following are guidelines I have written and followed over my sixteen years in the Air Force Band. I have modified them to cover those civilian buglers who may be called into service to sound "Taps" at funerals or memorial services. With the number of veteran funerals rising and the number of active-duty buglers declining, many nonmilitary musicians are asked to perform at the services.

1. Bugler is to prepare before the funeral, making sure to have the proper uniform and outerwear in case of inclement weather. Uniform, appearance, and instrument should meet or exceed the military standards as outlined in regulations. That is, make sure you look neat and presentable. A dark suit, quasi-military uniform, civilian band uniform, or Boy Scout uniform is acceptable. Retired military members can wear their uniforms.

2. Bugler is to report promptly to the funeral site at the appropriate time and report to the Officer in Charge (OIC) or Non-Commissioned Officer in Charge (NCOIC). If you are a civilian bugler performing at a military ceremony, always check in with that person to coordinate when "Taps" is to be sounded.

3. Bugler is to position himself near the gravesite, angled from the firing party. The bugler should take care to stand in a location where the sound will carry to the funeral party and where he can be seen. The bell of the instrument should be pointed toward the casket.

4. The bugler will render a Hand Salute as the casket is carried to the

gravesite. If you are in civilian dress, place your right hand over your heart. The bugler will stand at ease during the funeral service.

5. When the service is complete, the OIC or NCOIC will Present Arms. The firing party will come to attention and fire three volleys. Bugler will sound "Taps" after the third volley and after the NCOIC of the firing party executes Present Arms. After sounding "Taps," the bugler will render a Hand Salute and Order Arms on the command of the NCOIC of the firing party.

6. When a firing party is not available, the bugler will sound "Taps" on completion of the service and at an arranged signal by either the OIC, NCOIC, or officiating person. After sounding "Taps," the bugler will render a Hand Salute and Order Arms on his own. A recording of a firing party should not be used.

Performance Guidelines

1. The sounding of "Taps" at ceremonies is the most sacred duty a bugler can perform. Every effort should be made to sound a perfect "Taps" in keeping with the solemn and impressive occasion of a military ceremony.

2. The call should be sounded with conviction and not rushed. Every effort should be made to perform musically and with good intonation.

3. Careful attention should be paid to the rhythm of the seventh, eighth, tenth, eleventh, thirteenth, and fourteenth notes of "Taps" to ensure that they are played as straight eighth notes.

—*Master Sergeant Jari Villanueva, United States Air Force Band, Bolling Air Force Base, Washington, D.C.*

I also found out why I immediately thought of the plastic instrument as a "toy." The Army's new plastic bugles were distributed by the Chicago Musical Instrument Company and molded by the Elmer E. Mills Corporation, firms that made the popular toy plastic horns "Bugle Boy" and "Cadet Bugle."

The plastic bugle is the only major change in the design of the horn since valves were added, making it more like the modern-day trumpet, enabling it to play a wide variety of notes. The keyless bugle has a limited repertoire, such as "Taps" or "Reveille."

The history of the bugle is a long one, dating back some three thousand years to ancient Egypt. Some of the oldest bugles, or trumpets, still exist in museums today. Two of them, one silver and one bronze, each measuring more than two feet in length, were found in King Tutankhamen's tomb by explorer Howard Carter in 1922. Originally sounded in religious and state ceremonies, they now rest in silence at the Egyptian Museum in Cairo.

The spiritual influences of trumpets can be seen more recently in the Congo, where the Babwende tribe uses phallic-shaped trumpets in its funeral rites. And even today, in some regions of Switzerland, the bray of the enormous *Alpenhorn* echoes across the mountains as evening prayers are sung.

How did these wind instruments originate? As a child, you might have picked up a leftover cardboard wrapping paper tube and taken delight in amplifying your voice by talking through it. Most likely, the same discovery took place millennia ago when someone picked up a hollow tree branch and spoke or sang into it. Later someone discerned that by pressing his lips tightly against the end of a hollow branch—and blowing!—he could produce a loud, vibrant sound. And thus the horn was born. As the instrument became more sophisticated, it was discovered that by affixing an animal horn or hollow gourd at the end of the wooden tube, the sound was refined and further amplified.

Early musicians used other items—seashells and animal horns, for example—in the same manner. Because the conch shell is the home of a water animal, primitive people believed its sound exerted power over water and the moon and that the roar of the conch could bring—or stop—rain.

One instrument that appears in the Old Testament is still used today: the shofar has been used in Jewish ceremonies for more than three thousand years. Fashioned from a ram's horn, it is employed on special holidays.

Trumpets abound throughout the Bible. In the Book of Numbers, the Lord commands Moses to "Make thee two trumpets of silver; of a whole piece shalt thou make them: that thou mayest use them for the calling of the assembly, and for the journeying of the camps" (Numbers 10:2).

Historians point out that these ancient trumpets were not true musical instruments. The sound they produced was most likely harsh and toneless. In the fifth century B.C., the Greek historian Herodotus said that the noise made by Egyptian trumpet players sounded like the braying of an ass.

A bugle made of terra cotta, used in Rome in the fourth century A.D.

The trumpets of Moses, called *hatzotzeroth,* must have made an awful sound, for according to the Bible, when Joshua and his Israelite buglers played around the walls of Jericho, the walls fell down (Joshua 6:20).

During King Solomon's day, there were numerous job opportunities for trumpet players. It is estimated that 200,000 trumpet players lived in Israel during his reign. When Solomon's temple was consecrated, 120 trumpeters played "background" music.

Another biblical hero used trumpets against powerful Midianite enemies intent on destroying Israel. As Gideon prepared to go into battle, he knew that the enemy vastly outnumbered his three hundred troops. He gave each of his men a trumpet, and under cover of the darkness, they stole up to the enemy camp and blew their horns in unison. The Midianites, believing that only a huge army could make such a raucous noise, fled in confusion.

The Apostle Paul uses the instrument in a lesson on speaking clearly and forcefully: "For if the trumpet gives an uncertain sound, who shall prepare himself for the battle?" (I Corinthians 14:8).

Bugle is an old French word for "young bull," according to *The Trumpet Book* by Melvin Berger. The first bugle, made from the horn of a young bull, was called a bugle-horn.

Up until the end of the eighteenth century, bugles and trumpets were pretty much the same instrument: a cylindrical-tubed brass instrument with a mouthpiece and a bell. Also known as a "natural trumpet," when used in military practice it was referred to as a bugle; when employed otherwise (e.g., in an orchestra), it was a trumpet. The only way a player could change notes was via the manner in which he blew through the mouthpiece. Instrument manufacturers made trumpets in different keys, usually D or E.

In 1801, however, the first of many changes in bugle/trumpet design occurred: the development of what was called the "keyed bugle." This was a bugle with keys not unlike those you'll find on a saxophone. This was the first attempt to broaden the range of the instrument's tonality. However, the keyed bugle was not very effective; the keys produced an uneven, muffled sound and lacked the brassy blare of the original instrument.

In 1813, the keys were replaced with valves, and the instrument thus evolved into what is now known as the trumpet. The valves enabled the trumpeter to play a full scale in a comfortable and practical way and to produce much smoother-flowing notes. At this point in history the

The keyed bugle was a failed attempt to increase the range of the instrument. The keys were later replaced with the valves now present on trumpets.

trumpet became a more "musical" instrument and its use in orchestras greatly increased. The bugle remained, and continues to remain, valveless, with its comparatively limited five-

I was a high school student in St. Peter, Minnesota (pop. 7,000), from 1950 to 1954, and played trumpet in my high school band. I was also a Boy Scout, and earned a merit badge in bugling, so I knew many bugle calls in addition to "Taps." As my skill became known in the community, I was asked several times over the years to play "Taps" during veterans' burial ceremonies. These ceremonies were organized by the local VFW and American Legion branches, and were always moving occasions for me.

Most of the funerals at that time were for veterans of World War I. As the casket was lowered into the ground, fellow veterans would fire a salute with their rifles, and then I would play "Taps." Sometimes there would be two of us as buglers; one would play at graveside, and the second, standing behind a tree a hundred feet or so distant, would play an echo. Sometimes I was the principal player, but I actually preferred to play the echo, because it was more haunting, more moving, and I would get goose bumps—whether I was playing or listening—during the echo.

Although many years have passed since then, some of my most powerful and nostalgic memories are associated with those occasions.

—James M. McPherson, Edwards Professor of American History, Princeton University; author of Battle Cry of Freedom

note range. And what of the "keyed bugle"? It became obsolete.

It is worthwhile to note that although the bugle is popularly considered a "military" instrument and the trumpet an "orchestral" instrument, both are included in military bands and orchestras, and *both* are used for the playing of "Taps."

The U.S. military did not always use bugles to signal commands. In the 1700s, the fife and drum amplified the leader's orders. The trouble was that during battle drumbeats were often mistaken for the sound of musket fire.

As battlefields grew larger and troop numbers increased, shouted orders accompanied by fife and drum no longer sufficed. And so the bugle's blare was summoned to military duty.

There are many formal bugle calls that serve as the "chimes" of a military camp's clock, ranging from "Assembly of Buglers" and "Reveille" to "Taps," the final call of the day. Some of these calls, such as "Stable Call," have been dropped from use as the military becomes more modern.

An interesting reminiscence about these calls was written by Elizabeth Custer, wife of General George Armstrong Custer, in her book *Following the Guidon,* published fourteen years after her husband's death at Little Big Horn in 1876. In this passage she tells of life on the Army post:

> Before beginning the story of our summer's camp on Big Creek, Kansas, I should like to make our bugle a more familiar friend to those who know it only by hearsay. It was the hourly monitor of the cavalry corps. It told us when to eat, to sleep, to march, and to go to church. Its clear tones reminded us, should there be physical ailments, that we must go to the doctor, and if the lazy soldier was disposed to lounge about the company's barracks, or his indolent officer to loll his life away in a hammock on the gallery of his quarters, the bugle's sharp call sum-

moned him to "drill" or "dress parade." It was the enemy of ease, and cut short many a blissful hour. The very night was invaded by its clarion notes if there chanced to be fire, or should Indians steal a march on us, or deserters be discovered decamping. We needed timepieces only when absent from garrison or camp. The never tardy sound calling to duty was better than any clock, and brought us up standing; and instead of the usual remark, "Why, here it's four o'clock already!" we found ourselves saying: "Can it be possible? There's 'Stables,' and where has the day gone?"

The horses knew the calls and returned from grazing of their own accord at "Recall" before any trooper had started; and one of them would resume his place in the ranks, and obey the bugle's directions as nonchalantly as if the moment before he had not lifted a recruit over his head and deposited him on the ground.

Many Civil War commanders had their own unique "trademark" calls to precede a command signal so men in nearby regiments would know when a call did—and did not—apply to them.

Skilled buglers on the battlefield would often relay calls from other buglers. In fact, an expert bugler could "translate" the bugle calls of the enemy forces and keep his commander aware of their plans.

WHERE DID THE WORD TAPS ORIGINATE?

There are different theories regarding the origin of the title "Taps." The tune from which "Taps" was derived, "Tattoo," had been used as the Army's "Extinguish Lights" bugle call. "Tattoo" was a derivation of the Dutch term *Tap Toe*, which was a drumbeat used at military stations to warn local tavern keepers to close up their taps so that soldiers could return to their barracks.

A 1701 British army drill book states: "The tattoo or Taptoe; used in Garrisons or upon the Rounds to warn both the Soldiers and the inhabitants when they ought to repair to their Quarters." In the United States, *Duane's Handbook for Infantry*, published in 1812, states: "The sergeants and corporals call the roll at Taptoe time."

Another version is that "Tattoo" or "Taptoe" was derived from the Dutch words *tap toe* (meaning to turn the tap "to," or off). When it was time for soldiers to return to quarters, a drummer would parade through town beating out a warning. Tavern keepers would then "doe den tap toe," or turn the taps off.

Then there is the explanation that tattoo was a signal devised during the Thirty Years War (1618–1648) by Imperial General Albrecht von Wallenstein to get his men back to their camps at night. In the seventeenth-century German army, this hour was called *Zapfenstreich*, a time when tavern keepers drew a chalk line (a *streich*) across the tap (*zapfen*) as a kind of official marker, to be left intact until the opening of the tap the next day.

WHY THREE RIFLE VOLLEYS AT FUNERALS?

Before "Taps" is sounded at a military burial, three rifle volleys are usually fired. This custom dates back to the days when armies would call a cease-fire in order to clear their dead

Before the advent of powered amplification, other means were used to make sure that sailors heard their wake-up calls in the morning.

from the battlefield. Once the cleanup was complete, three rifle volleys were fired to signal that combat could resume.

Today, electronic recordings have replaced live bugle calls at many military posts. But undoubtedly, electronic or live, the

Buglers of Note

Many buglers throughout U.S. history have served with distinction. Among them are those who earned the Congressional Medal of Honor:

- John Cook, Fourth Artillery at Antietam, Maryland, September 17, 1862. As a young lad of fifteen, he saw the urgent need for cannoneers and volunteered to serve a gun while under terrific enemy fire.
- Richard Enderlin, Seventy-third Ohio Infantry at the Battle of Gettysburg, July 1–3, 1863. Enderlin voluntarily took a rifle and served in combat during the first and second days of the battle. He also voluntarily, and at his own imminent peril, went behind enemy lines at night and, under sharp fire, rescued a wounded comrade.
- James P. Landis, First Pennsylvania Cavalry, Pains Crossroads, Virginia, April 5, 1865. Landis captured the enemy flag, an extremely perilous action and always a tremendous blow to an opponent's morale.
- Charles W. Reed, Massachusetts Light Artillery, Gettysburg, Pennsylvania. July 2, 1863. Reed rescued a wounded captain from behind the lines and brought him to safety.
- Ferdinand F. Rohm, Sixteenth Pennsylvania Cavalry, Reams Stations, Virginia, August 25, 1864. While his regiment was retiring under fire, Rohm voluntarily remained behind to succor a wounded officer who was in great danger, secured assistance, and removed the officer to a place of safety.

- Charles Schorn, First West Virginia Cavalry, Appomattox, Virginia, April 8, 1865. Schorn captured the flag of the Confederate Sumter Flying Artillery.
- Thomas M. Wells, Sixth New York Cavalry, Cedar Creek, Virginia, October 19, 1864. Wells captured the colors of the Confederate Forty-fourth Georgia Infantry.

Others in the great tradition of bugling worthy of honor are:

- Gustav Schurmann, a twelve-year-old youth who served two Civil War generals and befriended Tad Lincoln, the president's son.
- Louis Benz, a native of Prussia who left his homeland and served as chief bugler at West Point for forty years.
- John Martin, George Custer's bugler and the last American soldier to see Custer alive. Born Giovanni Martini, he had changed his name so as to appear "more American."
- Frank Witchey, known for his rendition of "Boots and Saddles," which became a great favorite with cavalrymen. Witchey sounded "Taps" for the World War I Unknown Soldier during the burial ceremony at Arlington on November 11, 1921.
- Calvin Titus, a bugler during the siege of Peking in the Boxer Rebellion at the end of the nineteenth century in China. He responded to a call for volunteers to scale a wall with the now historic Army phrase "I'll try, sir!"
- George Myers, who bugled for "Black Jack" Pershing, Hap Arnold, Jonathan Wainwright, and at the interment of the World War II and Korean Unknown Soldiers. He considered the sounding of "Taps" to be the greatest of honors.

- Patrick Maestroleo, who sounded "Taps" for the interment of the Unknown Soldier of the Vietnam War.
- Jari Villanueva, master sergeant, United States Air Force Band. A musician and scholar, Villanueva has probably done more than anyone else in researching the history of the bugle and its role in the military.

most appreciated bugle call is the one described by a World War I doughboy in his letter home:

"Call to Quarters" blows, and soon "Taps" will lay us to rest for this day. As surely as the bugle calls of the day (save "Mess Call" and "Pay Call") are to be damned, those of the night are to be blessed. Particularly "Taps." No matter how a man wearies of this army, here is one call he wouldn't mind hearing every night his life through. It seems to us something more than beautiful music. In a way it symbolizes and humanizes this army that rides your neck all day, whispering at night that, after all, the army wishes you well, and that it's all for the good of the service. There are men who, if they go to bed before it sounds, lie awake and await it, much as the devout await Benediction. The grind, the disgust, the oath, the spur—these it obliterates, saying all our prayers for us and sending us quietly to sleep, better ready for another day.

CHAPTER FIVE

Lasting Monuments

THE MEMORIAL THAT PLAYS "TAPS"

Perhaps the most unusual memorial to "Taps" is the marker that has been erected on the very spot of its birth, Harrison's Landing, on the grounds of Berkeley Plantation in Virginia. As you stand on the peaceful grassy hill overlooking the shimmering James River, it's difficult to imagine this was once a muddy morass strewn with bloodied exhausted soldiers racked by disease and tortured by vicious biting flies. Groomed boxwood hedges and benches for visitors' comfort at the monument are in stark contrast to the offal and slit trenches that once befouled the air.

Now a breeze from the James fills the air with a fresh scent of flowers as you read the bronze plaque that summarizes the history of "Taps." But there is more. . . . Look for the special button on the memorial.* Press it and the sound of a bugler playing "Taps" echoes across the land. It's a moving experience, especially because you're listening to the notes where Private Oliver Willcox Norton first sounded them in 1862.

*Presented by the American Legion of Virginia.

In recent years, ragged and moldy military uniforms have been dug up from the ground around the monument. Union soldiers buried the tattered clothes in 1862 when General McClellan arrived from Washington bearing new uniforms for the weary troops.

It is worth noting that were it not for a young drummer boy who served under General McClellan, there would be no memorial at Harrison's Landing at all. He was John Jamieson, a Scottish lad with the Army of the Potomac. Stationed at Berkeley Plantation in 1862,

This monument to the origin of "Taps" lies on the grounds of the Berkeley Plantation in Charles City, Virginia.

he was one of those who heard the first sounding of "Taps." At the time, the plantation featured a lovely manor house, where wounded Union soldiers were lodged. To the young Jamieson, living in the squalor of the camps, the manor house was his idea of heaven. As he marched away with McClellan's Army, he vowed to return one day and live in the mansion.

Forty-five years later he made good on his promise. In his late fifties and a successful businessman, Jamieson returned and purchased the house and fourteen hundred surrounding acres. The years since the end of the Civil War had not been kind to the structure. It had stood empty all that time, exposed to the elements. The elegant woodwork had rotted away, the stonework had crumbled nearly to dust, and the beautiful gardens had been overrun by weeds. The cost of restoring the house and property proved too much for Jamieson, and so, twenty-five years later, when his son, Malcolm, inherited the property, it was still in ruins.

Malcolm, however, was bound and determined to succeed where his father had failed. He immediately set to work clearing the land and replanting trees, shrubs, and flowers. In 1933, he married Grace Eggleston, a talented interior designer. Together, the couple restored the house and grounds to the showplace it is today. The first floor of the manor house is open to the public; it features furniture dating from the

The beautiful manor house at Berkeley Plantation has been lovingly restored to its original condition.

mid-1860s as well as Chinese porcelain, English silver, and Waterford crystal from the period.

One element of the house has been left unrestored: a black iron cannonball fired by Confederate general J. E. B. Stuart's artillery in 1862 remains embedded in the wall of the old kitchen and laundry.

The Jamiesons still own and operate Berkeley Plantation, which is now a registered National Historic Landmark.

Thousands of people visit Berkeley Mansion annually. It is located at 12602 Harrison Landing Road, in Charles City, Virginia, halfway between Richmond and Williamsburg on historic Route 5. (Phone: 1-888-466-6018. Website: www.berkeleyplantation.com)

"TAPS" IN STAINED GLASS

The first sounding of "Taps" at a soldier's funeral is memorialized in a beautiful stained-glass window at the Chapel of the Centurion, also known as the Old Post Chapel, at Fort Monroe, Virginia. It commemorates the burial of a cannoneer in Captain John C. Tidball's artillery, killed during the Peninsular Campaign of 1862. The captain, concerned that the customary three rifle volleys fired over the grave would alert the nearby enemy to the presence of his troops, had the new call "Taps" sounded in their stead.

As you stand inside the chapel (the oldest wooden military chapel in the United States) and gaze at the window, the glowing colors portray a Union bugler under an American flag at half-mast. Dedicated in 1958, the window was designed by

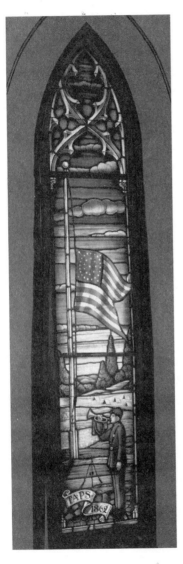

Colonel Eugene Jacob and made in New York by R. Geissler.

The window is based on a painting by Sidney King. In the original painting, a young drummer boy stands beside the bugler—this boy is John Jamieson, who returned decades later to purchase Berkeley Plantation.

WHERE "TAPS" IS HEARD MORE THAN ANYWHERE ELSE

In the rolling parkland of Arlington National Cemetery, across the Potomac River from Washington, D.C., a quarter-million American servicemen and -women are buried as well as two U.S. presidents: William Howard Taft and John Fitzgerald Kennedy. From a hill, the

The beautiful "Taps" stained-glass window can be found in the Chapel of the Centurion in Fort Monroe, Virginia. It is based in part on the painting by Sidney King.

gracious Greek-columned former mansion of Confederate general Robert E. Lee looks down upon those who sleep beneath the white markers.

Here, "Taps" is sounded more often than anywhere else on earth, as every weekday twenty to thirty military funerals are conducted with honors. The twenty-four notes that echo over the graves representing every state symbolize the unification of our country.

"Taps," of course, sounds at veterans' graves in all kinds of cemeteries around the country, and it is doing so in ever-increasing numbers as more than one thousand World War II veterans die every day. According to the Veterans Administration, which makes grave markers available for veterans, the Department of Defense will provide military funeral honors for eligible veterans upon their family's request. (For more

Freshly fallen snow blankets the grounds of Arlington National Cemetery. These partic-ular headstones mark the graves of many Civil War soldiers.

information, contact your local Veterans Affairs office or American Legion Post or VFW.) The above-mentioned honors include the playing of "Taps," though sometimes only a taped rendition of the song is available.

When the daughter of one World War II veteran was told that a tape would be played at her father's funeral, she reacted with righteous indignation. She is Cate Remme, of Anchorage, Alaska, whose father was Frederick "Fritz" Niland, a U.S. Army paratrooper with the 101st Airborne Division, who parachuted behind enemy lines in Normandy on June 5, 1944, the eve of D day. According to Remme, her father was a real-life counterpart of the hero of the Spielberg film *Saving Private Ryan*. In 1944, when his three brothers were listed as dead or MIA, Frederick Niland was ordered home by presidential edict. Franklin D. Roosevelt had ruled that no family should suffer the loss of more than two sons. So on July 13, 1944, Army Chaplain Father Francis Sampson sat down with Sergeant Niland, who had already learned that he had lost his three brothers. When the chaplain told him he was being sent home, Niland balked. "You tell my mother I'm with the only brothers I have left."

"You can take that up with General Eisenhower or the president," answered the chaplain. "But you're going home."

And so Fritz Niland traveled home, much to his mother's relief. Assigned to the train station in Buffalo, New York, as a military police officer, he found it difficult to be away from his combat buddies. Once, while in civilian clothes in a restaurant, he was approached by a stranger who demanded, "What's a healthy young man like yourself doing out of uni-

I had heard "Taps" played on television, but I'd never experienced it in real life until June of 2000 when my husband, Joseph, passed away. He'd been in the Navy for over twenty years and was very much a "flag-waver," as he would call himself. He often said that "freedom has a taste the protected will never know."

The day my husband was buried at Arlington is a day forever burned in my mind. As I stood there with family and friends, I could see a lone bugler off in the distance. I knew he was going to play "Taps" at the end of the service. When he began to play, my heart started to weep inside and I thought it would burst out of my chest. I cried even harder hearing that haunting

EM1 Joseph A. Harris, USN

melody. I felt that "Taps" both honored and bid good-bye at the same time to an individual who had served his country with pride and dignity.

And now my twenty-two-year-old son David is also in the Navy, serving in the Middle East and, as his father did, fighting in the name of freedom.

—*Sandra Harris,*
North Beach, Maryland

form?" Niland answered ironically: "I guess that's my reward for minding my own damn business."

After the war, Niland attended college at Georgetown on

the GI Bill and became an oral surgeon, got married, and became the proud father of two daughters.

"Dad did everything possible to help us realize the importance of the values he had fought for," said daughter Cate. " 'Hatred,' he said, 'is one of the most poisonous diseases afflicting humankind.' We already knew how it had killed some six million Jews in Europe. And we shuddered remembering how Dad's mother suffered from hatred during the war. While her four sons were away fighting for their country, some cruel neighbors hung her little dachshund from a tree in her backyard because it was a 'German' dog.

"Dad couldn't even hate the soldiers he fought," said Cate. "He had a healthy respect for them. 'They were brave men and good fighters,' he told us.

"He taught us to always stand up for right. When I was five, he took me out into the garage and taught me how to box. 'Don't go looking for trouble,' he cautioned, 'but you should know what to do if someone drops trouble in your pocket.' "

Sadly, Niland's own wartime experiences came to haunt him as the years went on. The deaths of two of his three brothers had been traumatic. On learning of the loss of his brother Robert in the D day invasion, he tried to find his body at one of the temporary cemeteries scattered around the Normandy area. He and a chaplain drove all day, searching the countryside. Finally, at one of the last burial grounds, the chaplain read through the list of the dead buried there. "The only Niland buried here is a Preston Niland," he concluded.

"That's how Dad found out that his other brother had also been killed," said Cate.

Fortunately, his third brother, Ed, listed as missing in the Pacific, actually survived his plane crash. Captured by the Japanese, he came close to death in a prisoner-of-war camp, but he escaped and was rescued by British troops.

"Despite [my father] having his brother Ed back again, the toll of past anxieties and sorrows caught up with [him]," said Niland's daughter. "In later years he suffered post-traumatic stress and bouts of depression—in 1983, at the age of sixty-three, he died from a heart attack."

By then Cate was living in Anchorage.

We tried to get his ashes buried in the Fort Richardson Military Cemetery, without success. Finally, one day while on the phone with a captain who kept saying, "Sorry, no room," I shot back, "You know, Captain, my father and his brothers would have made room for you on a certain flight to France one night . . . that is, if you would have had the guts to get on the plane."

A half hour later a man appeared at our door with the necessary papers. However, when the day arrived for [my dad's] burial, I found there would be no honor guard. I remembered with dismay being present at an earlier Vietnam combat vet's interment when "Taps" was played on a hiss-filled tape recording. I refused to continue with the ceremony until it could be conducted properly. Finally, on June 6th, 1985, the forty-first anniversary of D day, my father was buried with full military honors.

Even so, as we sat at the graveside with the bugler's haunting rendition of "Taps" echoing over the white markers, I prayed that my father's generation, who gave of themselves so unstintingly, would be remembered in some real way.

Then the phone call came.

It was Mark Bando, a historian of the 101st Airborne Division. "Has Hollywood called you yet?" he asked. "Steven Spielberg is making a movie called *Saving Private Ryan,* and the story is incredibly close to your father's."

A few weeks later we got a call from Bonnie Curtis, coproducer of the film. She said that it was a composite story of a number of families who had lost several brothers in the war. Knowing that the producers were not fully aware of my father's experience, I suggested that they talk to Stephen Ambrose, who had written about Frederick Niland in his military histories.

A short time later Bonnie Curtis invited our whole family to come to Hollywood to be a part of a television special on the film. On checking further, Steven Spielberg had pretty well figured out that it was the story of our family. We went late in June, thinking we'd only have a few minutes with Mr. Spielberg. Instead, he spent a whole hour with us. We learned his own father was a World War II combat veteran.

One of the scenes in the film that surprised me was when Private Ryan, told he was being sent home, replied in an eerie echo of my father's words: "You tell my mother I'm with the only brothers I have left."

I asked Mr. Spielberg, "How did you know my father refused to come home? That isn't in the history books; it's something only our family knew."

Spielberg's eyes widened behind his glasses. "Fate, is all I can say," he said. "It's something we wrote into the script figuring that's what he'd do." He sat back and added, "As an old saying goes, 'There's God's plan and there's man's plan, and man's plan doesn't matter.' "

Back in Arlington National Cemetery, the one place where "Taps" is heard most often is the Tomb of the Unknown Soldier, one of the most visited shrines in our nation's capital.

In the late 1970s, my wife and I were invited to attend a Memorial Day ceremony there. We will never forget it. It was a cool, cloudy day, and as we sat on the amphitheaterlike steps among the large crowd, I was touched to see the many foreign tourists who had taken the time to pay their respects to America's war dead.

As I looked at the white Vermont marble tomb, so grand and dignified in its simplicity, I thought of the story of how the unknown soldiers resting within had been chosen. After the guns of World War I had fallen silent, Congress decided that the body of an unknown soldier would be honored for the first time in a special tomb in Washington.

On Memorial Day of 1921, four unidentified bodies were

exhumed from four different American cemeteries in France. Placed in identical sealed caskets, they were carried into the city hall in Châlons-sur-Marne, France. One of these would be designated the Unknown Soldier.

A U.S. Army sergeant was given the honor of making the selection. He was Edward F. Younger, wounded combat veteran of "the Great War," who wore the Distinguished Service Medal. Carrying a spray of fresh white roses, he stepped alone into the quiet hall.

Who knows what thoughts went through his mind as he stood in that lonely place beside the four coffins. On which one would he place the roses? He was unaware of the race, color, or religion of any of the dead soldiers. We do know that he said he felt strongly moved to place the spray on top of one particular coffin. He then saluted and left. The other three were reinterred in the Meuse Argonne Cemetery.

The selected Unknown was carried to the soldier's homeland on the aft deck of the historic battleship USS *Olympia*, former flagship of naval hero Admiral George Dewey. The coffin lay in state in the Capitol Rotunda until Armistice Day 1921. On that day President Warren G. Harding officiated at the interment at Arlington National Cemetery.

Today, that Unknown Soldier is joined by fellow soldiers from World War II and the Korean War. There will probably never be another Unknown Soldier because today we have DNA testing. In fact, in 1998, the Vietnam Unknown was identified as Air Force First Lieutenant Michael Joseph Blassie, shot down in 1972. He was reburied at the military cemetery at Jefferson Barracks near St. Louis, Missouri. As they removed Blassie's coffin from the tomb, the U.S. Army Band performed "Goin' Home," a soulful arrangement by U.S. Air Force Master Sergeant Jari A. Villanueva.

When my wife and I attended the Memorial Day ceremonies in the late seventies, another Vietnam veteran was officiating:

A wreath-laying ceremony at the Tomb of the Unknown Soldier in Arlington National Cemetery.

Max Cleland, then head of the Veterans Administration and currently a U.S. senator from Georgia. A triple amputee, having lost both legs and an arm in a grenade explosion in Vietnam, he addressed the gathering from his wheelchair.

An old friend of our family, Max had invited Betty and me to the ceremonies. He was writing his autobiography, *Strong at the Broken Places,* and he and I spent a lot of time discussing it. He told me about his ancestors who fought for the Confederacy in the Civil War and how one of them had lost an arm in battle.

As "Taps" sounded that cloudy morning, I thought of how that call, which was so quickly adopted by both the Union and Confederate armies, unifies us today. That brothers, once separated by ideological differences so strong that 600,000 of them died fighting, could come together in friendship gave me hope that our current conflicts could be resolved peacefully.

Those Civil War enemies did come together in an astounding demonstration of friendship one hot July day some years after the war was over. I'll always remember Cleland's story about a memorable reunion at Gettysburg of soldiers from both the North and the South. The two sides decided to reenact Pickett's Charge, the famous action in which hundreds of Confederate men advanced across a wheat field to face Union soldiers emplaced at a stone wall. It was a maelstrom of musket fire, cannon explosions, and bloodied bayonets. General Pickett's men reached the wall in intense hand-to-hand combat but were almost annihilated and forced to withdraw. The wheat field and stone wall were strewn with dead and dying soldiers. It is said that this charge was the turning point in that day's battle. General Pickett himself never recovered emotionally from it.

Understandably, the reunion organizers felt some trepidation when the reenactment was proposed. What would happen when these men, still on fire with the cause for which they had fought, again met their former enemies at the same stone wall?

With this concern, they watched as the Confederate veterans began marching across the wheat field, the former Union men waiting silently behind the wall. No one spoke, no one cheered; no sound was heard except for the swish of shoes on grass as the Southern men advanced.

Then, as the Southern veterans neared the Union emplacement, an astonishing thing happened. The Northern men leaped over the wall and rushed toward their brothers, who now ran to them. In one long agonized cry they fell into one another's arms, overcome with emotion.

Lost in recollection of Max's story, I looked up to see him wheeling forward for the placing of the memorial wreath. Tears burned my eyes as I heard Japanese and German spoken in the crowd around me. I gave thanks that my World War II generation had also come together in peace and fellowship.

Betty and I left the Tomb of the Unknown that morning in silence, the lone sentry behind us pacing his cadenced step back and forth, back and forth, honoring all those who had died, from the men in homespun uniforms who fell on Lexington Green to those, God forbid, who may die for us in the future.

As we walked back to our car, we stopped at the resting place of President John F. Kennedy, with its eternal flame flickering over his grave. As we stood in contemplation, I thought back to that cold November 25, 1963, when "Taps" was played here at his funeral. And I remembered the "broken note," one of the most talked-about and misunderstood aspects of that ceremony.

THE BROKEN NOTE

The "Taps" that sounded at President Kennedy's funeral was probably heard by more people than any other rendition, thanks to its worldwide broadcast. According to William Manchester (author of *The Death of a President*), there were so many details demanding attention that grief-filled weekend that not until early in the morning of the state funeral did someone realize that no one had requested a bugler.

It was decided that thirty-six-year-old Sergeant Keith Clark, a trumpet soloist with the United States Army Band ("Pershing's Own"), stationed at nearby Fort Myer, Virginia, would do the honors. After graduating from Interlaken Music School and playing with the Grand Rapids Symphony, he had

joined the Army in 1946. According to Manchester, when Clark's children came home from school that day in November and shouted that the president had been assassinated, he guessed that Kennedy would be laid to rest in Arlington and that he would be the likeliest candidate to play "Taps." He then rushed out to his barber for a haircut.

Sergeant Keith Clark plays "Taps" at John F. Kennedy's grave in Arlington National Cemetery.

Clark had sounded "Taps" at hundreds of funerals in Arlington National Cemetery; he'd played for President Eisenhower and Vice President Nixon. Only two weeks earlier, on Veterans Day, he had played "Taps" at the Tomb of the Unknown Soldier as President Kennedy looked on.

About 1:30 on the morning of the funeral, he was awakened by a phone call from his commander telling him that he would be playing "Taps" at the ceremony. Sergeant Clark reported to Arlington in full-dress uniform at 5:40 A.M., only to discover that he and the men who were spraying the fall-seared grass green were the only ones there. After waiting in the thirty-degree cold for two hours, he returned to Fort Myer in a vain attempt to get more sleep. At 9:00 A.M. his phone rang; he had missed the rehearsal of the graveside ceremonies.

"Report to the cemetery at noon," he was told. He went home to catch some of the funeral on television and returned to the gravesite at 11:50 A.M. Someone showed him the microphone into which he was to play. It was far too close. "I'm not playing for the mike," he said. "I'm playing for Mrs. Kennedy."

Then Sergeant Clark waited another tension-filled three hours in the cold—the bane of all brass players—until the funeral Mass ended at St. Matthew's Cathedral in downtown Washington, D.C. A deeply religious man, he reflected on some of his favorite hymns and Bible passages as he ate an apple for lunch. He cradled his bugle in his hands because the pitch varies with the temperature. Finally, he watched the funeral procession approach, led by the U.S. Marine Band, followed by troops from all branches of the military, the Air

I served as an airborne Ranger platoon leader (paratrooper) in the First Air Cavalry Division during the Vietnam War.

Our company was hacked up pretty badly by the enemy during one mission. When our platoon's survivors returned to base camp, we all trudged down the muddy path to our tent. As the men took their places in their bunks, the number of empty bunks became apparent. Men put their faces in their hands and sobbed liked children. Each of us wondered if our bunk would be empty at the end of the next mission.

Fortunately, there was something we could always count on to help keep our sanity . . . late in the evening, long after the sun had gone down, a distant bugle could be heard playing "Taps." When that haunting and nostalgic song was played, all activity in the battalion area came to a screeching halt. Conversation would stop and men would sit back in their bunks, listening to what had to be the most poignant sound I have ever heard.

Now, years later, as I look back on the horrors of that combat, I remember that unknown bugler who played "Taps" so late every night. It seemed that, if only for a few moments, we were assured that someone was up there, sending us renewed hope through those twenty-four simple notes.

So many men in our unit didn't make it back home alive. I needed to write this for those who did.

—*Bill Scheibler, Vietnam veteran,*
Eden Prairie, Minnesota

Force Band, the coffin-bearing caisson pulled by six white horses, and finally Black Jack, the ebony horse with empty boots facing backward in their stirrups.

A little before 3:00 P.M., the Kennedy family and assorted dignitaries stood at the gravesite as the band played. Fifty jet fighters roared overhead, along with Air Force One, and Cardinal Cushing completed the burial rites.

As the twenty-one-cannon salute thundered across the graves of Arlington, Sergeant Clark stood with his bugle at the ready. Then, after three rifle volleys rang out, only ten paces away, Clark, now deafened by the rifle blasts, raised his bugle and pointed the bell in the direction of Jacqueline Kennedy. Words from I Corinthians 15:51–52 came to his mind: ". . . we shall all be changed, in the twinkling of an eye, at the last trumpet . . ."

"Day is done . . ." he began playing. "Gone the . . ." As he started to play the sixth note, his bugle "cracked," as can happen to all brass players. "It was like a catch in your voice, or a swiftly stifled sob," wrote Manchester. Sergeant Clark recovered from the error and finished the call perfectly.

Many in the audience thought the cracked note was deliberate. *Newsweek* magazine called it a "tear," and one writer for *TV Guide* wrote, "The bugler's lip quivered for the Nation."

Washington Magazine, in reporting that the broken note took on a life of its own, said: "To many Americans, spent from four days of mourning, it captured the nation's heartache over a beloved young president's death."

"I missed a note under pressure," said Clark as we talked about his experience. "As I tried to hold that flat-ish sixth note up into pitch, it got away from me. It's something you don't like, but it's something that can happen to any trumpet player. You never really get over it."

For weeks afterward, other Arlington buglers cracked the same note, said Clark. "We all thought it must be psychological."

In 1977, Sergeant Clark retired from the Army after twenty years of service and went on to a successful scholarly and writing career, including teaching music at Houghton College. He continued to perform as a trumpeter, however. The research he had done on hymns had earned him high recognition in his field as well as many awards. Keith Clark died at age seventy-four on January 11, 2002, after doing what he loved most, playing his trumpet at a recital. His obituary in the *New York Times* noted that his performance of "Taps" at John F. Kennedy's funeral "came to be seen as a perfect embodiment of national sorrow."

The bugle he played at the Kennedy funeral remains at Arlington National Cemetery, a centerpiece of the "Taps" exhibit.

THE "TAPS" EXHIBIT AT ARLINGTON

Located at the cemetery where "Taps" is heard more times than anywhere else, the exhibit *Taps—the Military Bugle in History and Ceremony*—may be found in the visitors' center. Opened in 1999, the exhibit is scheduled to close in September 2002. Its fascinating memorabilia include bugles from every era of the last two hundred years, historic photos, sheet music, manuals, uniforms, and bugler insignia.

The grave of President John F. Kennedy in Arlington National Cemetery is located below Arlington House, which was once the home of General Robert E. Lee.

It also includes the ornate duty sword of General Daniel Butterfield and his golden spurs, a gift from admiring officers for his leadership at the Battle of Hanover Court House in May 1862.

An excerpt from the moving invocation by Chaplain (Colonel) Edward Brogan at the opening of the "Taps" exhibit, May 28, 1999, illuminates the spirit of the famous bugle call:

> Lord of our lives, our hope in death, we cannot listen to "Taps" without our souls stirring. Its plaintive notes are a prayer in music—of hope, of peace, of grief, of rest. . . . Prepare us too, Lord, for our final bugle call when you summon us home! When the trumpet of the Lord shall sound and death will be no more.

"MR. 'TAPS' "

The creator of the Arlington "Taps" exhibit was Master Sergeant Jari A. Villanueva, who is with the United States Air Force Band at Bolling Air Force Base in Washington, D.C. It took him almost a year to assemble the exhibit with help from private collectors, institutions, historical societies, and items from his own extensive collection.

Master Sergeant Villanueva is practically a memorial to "Taps" himself. Perhaps the most noted authority on the call, he is also writing a book, *Day Is Done: A History of Bugles in the United States Military*.

For more than seventeen years Villanueva has sounded "Taps" at Arlington and other cemeteries. To his mind, the most important of these occasions were the many times he played at the Tombs of the Unknowns. To him this is the highest honor a bugler can perform, "the military musician's equivalent of playing Carnegie Hall." He has sounded "Taps" at the funerals of General Ira Eaker, World War II commander of the Eighth Air Force, and General Godfrey McHugh, Air Force aide to President John F. Kennedy. On every Memorial Day weekend for the past twelve years, he has performed a memorial service for the Flying Tigers, the legendary World War II flying group in China, at the Old Memorial Amphitheater at Arlington.

"To me," states Villanueva, " 'Taps' conveys an important message through its twenty-four notes. To U.S. soldiers from the Civil War on, when sounded at night, the call meant that all was well. It gave a sense of security and safety to those men

Master Sergeant Jari Villanueva is an expert on the role of the bugle in the U.S. Armed Forces as well as "Taps."

and also signaled that another day in the service to their country was done. Because of the melodious and poignant nature of the call it is no wonder that it was adopted as the final call at funerals. As Gustav Kobbé stated in an 1898 *Century* article, 'Played slowly and expressively, it has a tender, touching, mournful character, in keeping with the fact that it is sounded not only for "lights out," but also over the soldier's grave, be he general or private, so that as with "lights out" night closes in upon the soldier's day, so with the same call the curtain rolls down upon his life.' "

CHAPTER SIX

Setting Words to Music

Surprisingly, there are no official lyrics to "Taps." It was composed, after all, as a military bugle call, and such calls traditionally do not have words. Yet because the spirit of "Taps," eloquently conveyed by its haunting tune, touches the emotions so deeply, writers through the years have been inspired to create words to accompany its poignant notes. The assorted lyrics are all moving, each in their way, and range from simple words to lyric prayers. Oddly enough, none of these words have been attributed to any particular author.

TAPS

The musical notation for "Taps."

Most likely, the first to draft words to "Taps" were Civil War soldiers, since it was a popular practice among troops to attach words to bugle calls.

The first and most simple of the lyrics ascribed to "Taps" during the Civil War were:

> *Go to sleep,*
> *Go to sleep,*
> *Go to sleep, go to sleep, go to sleep,*
> *You may now*
> *Go to sleep,*
> *Go to sleep.*

Twenty-four notes, twenty-four words.

My daddy served in WWII and he died an old man at forty-four. I am his only daughter with five brothers. He was so proud of fighting for his country! I miss him desperately. The song "Taps" always brought tears to his eyes and pride in his broken heart. It's sad, but if "Taps" had never been written, I may have never witnessed tears in my daddy's eyes.

> *T is for my daddy's Tender heart for all;*
> *A is for Asking your country what you can do for her and doing it;*
> *P is for the Patriot my daddy so proudly hailed;*
> *S is for Soldier, because my daddy told me what it meant to be one.*

In loving memory of Freddie C. Chapple, my daddy, my hero.

—*Phyllis Perkins, Birmingham, Alabama*

There was a variation in which the words *Put out the lights* replaced *Go to sleep* (*put out* was doubled up onto the note for the word *go*).

It's easy to picture a thoughtful trooper attending a fellow soldier's burial, coining this closing verse:

> *'Tis thy reward*
> *Sleep ye sweet*
> *With thy God*
> *Rest be thine.*

Today, two of the best-known lyrics are:

Version One

> *Day is done,*
> *Gone the sun,*
> *From the lakes, from the hills, from the sky,*
> *All is well,*
> *Safely rest,*
> *God is nigh.*
>
> *Fading light,*
> *Dims the sight,*
> *And a star gems the sky, gleaming bright,*
> *From afar,*
> *Drawing nigh,*
> *Falls the night.*
> *Thanks and praise,*

For our days,
'Neath the sun, 'neath the stars, as we go,
This we know,
God is nigh,
God is nigh.

Then good night,
Peaceful night,
Till the light of the dawn shineth bright.
God is near,
Do not fear,
Friend, good night.

Version Two

Day is done,
Gone the sun,
From the hills, from the lake, from the skies,
All is well,
Safely rest,
God is nigh.

Go to sleep,
Peaceful sleep,
May the soldier, or the sailor, god keep.
On the land,
Or the deep,
Safe in sleep.

Love, good night,
Must thou go,
When the day and the night need thee so?
All is well,
Speedeth all,
To their rest.

Fades the light,
And afar,
Goeth day, and the stars shineth bright.
Fare thee well,
Day has gone,
Night is on.

Thanks and praise,
For our days,
'Neath the sun, 'neath the stars, 'neath the sky,
As we go,
This we know,
God is nigh.

"Taps," of course, plays a prominent role in both Boy and Girl Scout activities. At the close of official Scout ceremonies—for example, the Boy Scouts Court of Honor, in which new Scouts are received and awards are presented—"Taps" is played by a bugler. Often a second bugler will play an echo. (For more on the famous "Echo," see chapter 8.)

There is even a Merit Badge for bugling. It is earned by a Boy

NO. 8 "TATTOO"

The musical notation for "Tattoo." "Taps" is thought to have been derived from the last five and a half bars of this bugle call.

Scout who learns the history of the instrument, how it makes its sound, its relationship to other horns, and how to properly clean and maintain it. Further, the Scout must sound a wide variety of calls (including "Taps") and explain their meanings. Then he must serve as a troop bugler for three months.

Girl and Boy Scouts use the same version of "Taps." In the

Girl Scouts, the Scout "Taps" is usually sung as part of the closing of the Friendship Circle at the end of each Scout meeting. The Girl Scouts also have a "Daylight Taps," which is sung when concluding ceremonies are held during daylight hours instead of the evening.

Scout "Taps"

Day is done,
Gone the sun,
From the lake, from the hills, from the sky
All is well,
Safely rest,
God is nigh.

Fading light,
Dims the sight,
And a star gems the sky, gleaming bright.
From afar,
Drawing nigh,
Falls the night.

Thanks and praise,
For our days,
'Neath the sun, 'neath the stars, 'neath the sky,
As we go,
This we know,
God is nigh.

Sun has set,
Shadows come,
Time has fled, Scouts must go to their beds.
Always true,
To the promise
That they made.

While the light,
Fades from sight,
And the stars, gleaming rays softly send,
To Thy hands,
We our souls,
Lord, commend.

Another version of "Taps" is called "Canadian Taps." It's used by the Girl Guides, that nation's counterpart to the Girl Scouts.

"Canadian Taps"

Softly falls the light of day
As our camp fire fades away
Silently each one should ask
Have I done my daily task?
Have I kept my honour bright?
Can I guiltless sleep tonight?
Have I done and have I dared
Everything to Be Prepared?

Most people assume that "Taps" is played only at military funerals and ceremonies. In fact, the song is an integral part of many different ceremonies, including those of the Boy Scouts, summer camps, and police and fire department funerals, among others. "Taps" has been played at the funerals of many celebrities, including Buffalo Bill Cody, Oscar Hammerstein, and Rocky Marciano. As jazz great Louis Armstrong lay in state in Manhattan, the only music the family allowed to be played was "Taps."

Anyone trying to sing these lyrics to the tune of "Taps" had better "be prepared" himself, however—even though the song is called "Canadian Taps," it is actually set to the tune of the German Christmas carol "O Tanenbaum."

There are scores of other lyrics used in varied circumstances by different groups.

If I were to choose lyrics to accompany "Taps" played at a funeral, I would find this variation fitting:

Version Three

Fades the night,
And afar,
Goeth day, cometh night, and a star,
Leadeth all,
Speedeth all,
To their rest.

Love, good night,
Must thou go,

When the day and the night leave me so?
Fare thee well,
Day is done,
Night is on.

When your last,
Day is past,
From afar, some bright star o'er your grave,
Watch will keep,
While you sleep,
With the brave.

Today, "Taps" sounds all over the world. One can hear its notes played by a French army bugler; France adopted the song as its own military closing call in 1937. One American tourist was astounded to hear the familiar bugle call sound over the PA system of a German department store to signify closing time, perhaps inspired by the notes heard at a nearby U.S. Army post.

You can find the

A German Legionnaire plays "Taps."

words for "Taps" in many languages, including that of the Maori, the indigenous people of New Zealand:

Haere ra, E te ao,	*Farewell, To the light,*
E te tai, Te puke, Te rangi,	*To the sea, The hill, The sky,*
Ke te pai, Piri mai,	*All is well, Draws near,*
Te Atua	*The Lord.*

I've also found "Taps" translated into Dutch, German, Swedish, and Finnish, among others—a testament to its international appeal. In any language, "Taps" always touches our hearts. I believe this is because no matter our race, religion, or nationality, we respond to the sentiment conveyed in those twenty-four notes: the compassion of a thoughtful man for his suffering fellows, a compassion that resonates in the human soul.

As a child, I attended a Christian camp in rural Kentucky. Every night I would fall asleep to the sound of "Taps" floating through the hardwood forests around me. The frogs croaked a little louder, cicadas ratcheted up their chorus, and I drifted off into the magical land of dreams.

—*Philip Yancey, author*

CHAPTER SEVEN

"Taps" in Literature

s the emotional call of "Taps" was quickly woven into the fabric of military life, so has it resonated in literature, almost from the day it was first played.

One of the earliest literary references to "Taps" was made by Mark Twain in his novella *A Horse's Tale,* written in 1905. In the story, General Alison writes to his mother about a Western regiment playing farewell music for a visiting girl named Cathy. They run through standards such as "The Star-Spangled Banner," "Reveille," "Boots and Saddles," and finally, "Taps." Twain writes:

> Now an impressive pause—then the bugle sang "Taps"—translatable, this time into "Good-bye, and God keep us all!" for "Taps" is the soldier's nightly release from duty, and farewell; plaintive, sweet, pathetic, for the morning is never sure, for him; always it is possible that he is hearing it for the last time. . . .

In the early twentieth century, *Poetry* magazine carried this echo of the Great War:

TAPS

BY BAKER BROWNWELL

Into pure night
A strand of golden sound
Weaves a design.

Life woven in sound
Is night and song.
Pathos—of a soul—
Inspires the darkness.

One of the most recent works to include "Taps" is one titled after the song itself: *Taps*, a novel by the late Willie Morris, who also authored the notable books *My Dog Skip* and *North Toward Home*. As in his other works, *Taps* draws on the author's memories of life in a small Southern delta town.

It is 1951 when sixteen-year-old Swayze Barksdale watches the young men of Fisk's Landing, Mississippi, march off to a faraway place called Korea. Too young to serve overseas, Swayze is soon called to unexpected duty at home; a local boy is an early casualty of the war, and Swayze is enlisted to play "Taps" at his graveside. Gradually, Swayze begins to pace his life around these all too frequent funerals, where his trumpet sounds the musical accompaniment to the times.

The novel evokes daily life in Fisk's Landing, with its comforting rhythms, hilarious mishaps, and moments of pure joy. Young love blossoms and age-old hatreds flare anew as Swayze enters adulthood and learns what it means to be a patriot, a son, a lover, and a friend. Ultimately, when he must play "Taps" for someone he holds dear, Swayze learns what it means to be a man.

As it turned out, the "Taps" for Luke would be our last.

It was an overcast afternoon, much like the one nearly a year before when Luke had found the spot for my echo, with a hot breeze and muffled thunder and intermittent rain. The creamy white blossoms of my magnolia were warm to the touch and deeply scented. Luke had been such a part of these graveside rituals that I could hardly imagine not seeing him today.

In my dull, throbbing sorrow, as I waited alone under the tree with my trumpet, I withdrew the jack-knife Georgia had given me on my birthday and carved Luke's initials, then mine, into the bark, just as Miles Featherstone had done on the elm near the boulevard in 1901. You can visit the Fisk's Landing cemetery today and find this small gesture to immutability; long after the last mansion in Tara Estates has crumbled to ruin, it will surely remain. Gazing out at the familiar terrain and the old town there before me, I felt a haunted sense of endless earth, of inexhaustible and unremitting skies, of the heavens infinite and far away.

I grieved for Luke, and I knew in my inmost heart that I would live forever with my disgrace.

I served in the Navy during World War II from 1943 to 1944, attached to the 121st Seabee Battalion as a refrigerator repair engineer stationed on the island of Guam. A Navy friend had a dog, a part Boston terrier. I don't know where he found her, but she became the unofficial mascot of our battalion. In fact, she was awarded two ribbons of the Pacific Campaign as she was with the battalion during the Battle of Guam.

Her name was Lady. When it was time for my pal to ship back to the States, he asked if I would take care of her. I happily said yes, as Lady and I were great friends.

While onshore we lived in wooden barracks, each of which held ten to twelve men. At night, my shipmates and I would play cards, or lie on our bunks and talk, while Lady rested under my cot. When it came time for lights out, "Taps" would sound, and Lady jumped out from under my cot and curled up at my feet or by my side for the night. And every morning when "Reveille" sounded, Lady jumped up again, and made sure that the rest of us got going, too!

When it was time for me to be shipped home, I asked for and received permission to take Lady with me. So she got all her shots and off we went to the U.S.A. When we arrived in California, a

Al Cioffi wth Lady, Guam, 1944.

couple of friends met us to take me out for my first stateside meal. I couldn't wait to eat steak! Of course I brought Lady with me. But when we got to the restaurant the headwaiter told me that I couldn't take my dog into the dining room. I said, "But, sir, this dog is a veteran," and pointed to Lady's collar, to which I had attached her service ribbons. "In that case," he said, "go right on in."

I had Lady for another four years before she died. It broke my heart to lose such a dear friend, and I still think of her, especially when I hear "Taps" and remember how she kept me company when I was so far from home."

—Al Michael Cioffi, World War II veteran

It began to rain harder. Soon the cortege came, led by Potter in the new hearse. Luke's C.O. from New England was there; Georgia and Idella King and Asphalt Thomas had brought Amanda. The pageantry of the grave unfolded and was followed by Arch's "Taps."

As I started my echo, it came to me that what we really had been playing all that year was a song to everyone resting in this graveyard, to everyone I had ever cared for, to my own distant progeny, as if in all those months here and at Locust Grove and Blackjack and the river town on the bluffs, Arch and I had been carrying on a secret conversation, just between ourselves, and that I had been giving answer to his question, over the grave and beyond it, about death in life, about the passing generations in their own solicitudes, about flawed people and all their dark inheritance:

Day is done,
Gone the sun,
From the lake,
From the hills,
From the sky.
Rest in peace,
Soldier brave,
God is nigh.

The notes from my trumpet rose in the unresisting air, and I closed my eyes against the tears.

> In a word, "Taps" to me means "tribute" in the richest sense of the term. I have heard it played in tribute to fallen warriors and shipmates whose actions commanded the deepest respect. Whenever I hear the notes, under any circumstances, I am moved passionately. No other simple herald produces such a powerful effect.
>
> —*Admiral James M. Loy, Commandant,*
> *U.S. Coast Guard, 1998–2002*

Many other well-known authors have included "Taps" in their writing, among them James Jones in *From Here to Eternity,* F. Scott Fitzgerald in *Taps at Reveille,* and Jesse Stuart in *Taps for Private Tussie.*

There are also a number of "homegrown" authors, published either privately or on the Internet, who have written works dealing with "Taps." Following are two particularly effective pieces, one from poet Ann Cragg and one from Cadet Kelly Strong.

TAPS

BY ANN CRAGG

Through my kitchen window I can see it begin—
First snow of the season, third year in a row—
Flakes so big and beautiful I wish that I
Could catch a few and preserve them in a jar!
Whirling, swirling, dancing gracefully, gently,
The snowflake ballet is soon forced to the ground
By a snowfall growing much faster and harder;
No more gentle flakes whirling gracefully around!
Still I can see through the fast-falling curtain—
Can see one block north to the banner on high—
To the well-kept National Cemetery
Where men from the Civil and other Wars lie.
I can both see and hear each new burial—
The commands, the rifles' fire, the bugle's farewell.
How many books could be filled with the stories
That only those resting here could tell?
Beneath neat white headstones, row upon row—
They lie together now in a peaceful rest—
The sharply chiseled letters on the headstones
Telling the names of these bravest and best,
While the Stars and Stripes flies above them each day.
The snowflakes are now spreading a soft white pall
Over the graves of those who've served their country—

Have served and have fought and have given their all,
How many of the men who die in this War
Will be brought back here to be given a plot,
The rifles' salute and the bugle's sad Taps?
It seems so little, in return for such a lot . . .

Ann Cragg was twenty-five years old when those around her began to leave home in the service of their country. Here, she recounts what those days were like and how they inspired her heartfelt poem, "Taps."

Poet Ann Cragg, in 1994, after pulling an all-night shift at the ordnance plant. Note that she's wearing her plant badge and locker key.

The World War II years in the United States were a time of such patriotism as was never seen again in the twentieth century. Women gladly took jobs in shipyards, aircraft factories, ordnance plants—and worked long hours with the Red Cross. We dutifully saved our grease, gave up our nylons, and dealt with rationing—even of gasoline.

We were proud of our men in uniform. We wrote weekly letters to friends and daily letters to our loved ones. We tried to keep up a cheerful front but could not help worrying when alone.

I worked the graveyard shift at an ordnance plant, filling the little detonators with explosive powders. I loved my job and was proud to be doing my bit to help win the war.

We knew our men in England were preparing to cross the Channel and invade France, but we had no idea how soon it would come. We knew it was the only way to end the war and were resigned to the fact.

Our feelings were mixed, however. We wanted the war to be over as soon as possible, but at the same time, we knew we'd suffer extensive casualties.

So it was with a heavy heart that I watched the lovely snowfall that day and wondered: Would my loved one return safely to me—or fall, and come home to rest quietly beneath a white headstone?

The following poem is by an unknown author; all attempts to locate him or her have been fruitless. And, although it does not mention "Taps," you can almost hear those sad, soft strains as you read the anonymous poet's heartfelt verse.

EULOGY FOR A VETERAN

Do not stand at my grave and weep,
I am not there, I do not sleep.
I am a thousand winds that blow.
I am the diamond glints on snow.
I am the sunlight on ripened grain.
I am the Gentle autumn rain.
When you awaken in the morning hush,
I am the swift uplifting rush
of quiet birds in circled flight,

I am the soft stars that shine at night.
Do not stand at my grave and cry,
I am not there, I did not die.

When I was growing up, I used to go to a Boy Scouts camp on Loon Pond in Massachusetts, not too many miles away from my home in Brookline. My older brother was there with me for the four weeks during our summer vacation, but that didn't always dull the pain of homesickness, especially during that first summer. And beyond that, the eerie sounds emitted by the loons each night across the lake, a kind of mournful, drawn-out whistling lament did little to reassure me.

But then, come nine o'clock every night, "Taps" was blown by an older Scout and somehow, mysteriously, it never failed to settle me down. There was a kind of magic to it, a wonderfully reassuring sound that meant "Day is done . . . Go to sleep . . . You're safe and sound." I've never forgotten it.

—*Mike Wallace, senior correspondent,*
60 Minutes

Kelly Strong was an eighteen-year-old high school senior and Air Force JROTC cadet in Homestead, Florida, when he wrote the following poem in 1981. Since then he has received thousands of letters and e-mail messages from people around the country who expressed how much the poem touched their lives. He is currently a search and rescue and air intercept pilot in the Coast Guard.

FREEDOM IS NOT FREE

I watched the flag pass by one day—It fluttered in the breeze
A young marine saluted it—And then he stood at ease
I looked at him in uniform—So young, so tall, so proud
With hair cut square and eyes alert—He'd stand out in any crowd
I wondered how many men like him—Have fallen through the years
How many died on foreign soil—How many Mothers' tears
How many pilots' planes shot down—How many died at sea
How many foxholes were soldiers' graves—No, Freedom is not Free
I heard the sound of Taps one night—When everything was still
I listened to the bugler play—And felt a sudden chill
I wondered just how many times—Taps had meant "Amen"
When a flag had covered a coffin—Of a brother or a friend
I thought of all the children—of the Mothers and the Wives
Of Fathers, Sons, and Husbands—With interrupted lives
And I thought about the graveyard—At the bottom of the sea
Of unmarked graves in Arlington—No, Freedom is not Free.

Cdr. Kelly Strong, USCG
KellyStrong@aol.com

If "God Bless America" has become our second national
anthem, then "Taps" has become America's requiem for its
fallen heroes.

CHAPTER EIGHT

A Song of the American People

A FINAL FAREWELL

Memorial Day 2001 dawns hot and sunny in Rye, New York, a suburban town on the Long Island Sound, about twenty-five miles from New York City.

Sean Moynihan, eighteen-year-old Rye High School senior, blinks awake when his mother calls him. No school today, a holiday. But he has to get up anyway. He will be sounding "Taps" at the town's Memorial Day ceremonies on the village green.

The members of the Rye American Legion Post No. 128 have sponsored the Memorial Day ritual for more than fifty years. At this point there are roughly eighty members in the post, most of them veterans of World War II. They wish that more Korean and Vietnam War vets would join their ranks, as their membership is rapidly dwindling. After all, the last world war ended fifty-seven years ago. The attrition leaves fewer men to assist in conducting the Memorial Day and Veterans Day services, which are held in front of city hall alongside the plaque honoring those local men and women lost in service to their country.

The elderly Legion men with blue overseas caps are a bit stooped with years. Joints ache from arthritis, many take medication for heart problems—the list is long. Someday they'll all be gone. Who will handle the ceremonies then?

They start planning for Memorial Day early in the year. Someone has to solicit essays from local high school kids on "What America Means to Me." Someone else has to research and nominate a worthy local citizen for the Rye Americanism Award. And finally, someone has to round up a bugler to play "Taps."

Until about ten years ago, the sounding of "Taps" was simply a tape recording played over a loudspeaker. The men of the Rye American Legion felt that a live bugler would be a more fitting honor to their fallen comrades, however, so they made the rounds of the local school bands in search of a suitable trumpeter. (A bugler would be suitable, too, of course, but most high school bands do not have buglers, as the trumpet is a more versatile instrument.)

This year, Rye High School band director Dan Brown asks his students: "Who wants to play 'Taps' at the Memorial Day services?"

Most of the kids have plans for that Monday of the long weekend; Sean Moynihan is the only one who raises his hand. Maybe it's because his father, Tim, is a lieutenant colonel in the Air Force National Guard. Sean remembers his dad being gone for a long time during Desert Storm, Bosnia, and Afghanistan.

"Taps" is an integral part of the Boy Scout's ritual.

At eight o'clock that Monday morning he wishes he hadn't raised his hand. He has a big ball game that day and needs to get ready for it. He gets up, eats a dish of cold cereal, then opens the case holding his silver Bach trumpet. With a clean soft cloth he polishes it until he can see his face in its gleaming bell.

He arrives at the village green about nine forty-five in the morning. The Legion men breathe a sigh of relief, especially since someone has forgotten where the old tape of "Taps" is. Sean stands in the background, leaning against one of the oak trees. He watches the local dignitaries make their speeches: the mayor, the county legislator, the congresswoman, the ladies being honored with awards for wartime service.

Names of dead soldiers are read, men who should have been standing on the green today with their wives and grand-children.

Sean knows it all by heart; he has been attending these ceremonies since he was a child. But this will be his last—come September, he'll be off to Villanova University in Pennsylvania.

Finally, the old Legionnaires line up with the memorial wreaths to decorate the plaques and the flagpole. Their steps do not have the quick cadence they had on the parade ground more than fifty years earlier; sometimes they falter.

Then it's time. Sean lifts the trumpet to his lips. He sounds the twenty-four notes, over the village green, across the halted cars, over the heads of aging Gold Star mothers who lost a child in one of the World Wars, touching the hearts of everyone who hears them.

Sean thinks of family members who have served in

As National Commander of the American Legion, our nation's largest veterans' organization, I forlornly attend the burial ceremonies of too many of my fellow veterans who transfer to "Post Everlasting."

The striking sound of the rifle salute is always finalized with the resonant notes of "Taps." A bugler slowly wafts this final and moving harmony as a last testament to a fallen comrade. This comrade is an ordinary American who once answered the call of his or her country, and now, that of his or her Creator.

As the final salute to a fellow veteran, it is an expression of grief that brings a tear to one's eye and touches the depth of one's soul.

—*Richard J. Santos, National Commander, American Legion*

the armed forces. He remembers his grandfather, who carried a light machine gun through Europe. And his father, still with him, who never knows when he'll be called away to serve in the Air Force Reserves.

Sean has devised his own special way to play "Taps." He uses the number two and three valves on his E-flat trumpet. "That's the saddest sound I've ever heard," his bandleader remarks on hearing it. That's exactly the reaction Sean wants.

The final note drifts away. Sean cradles his trumpet by his side as he looks to the wall outside city hall and its long list of names. Silence hangs over the green. No one moves for a moment. And then the crowd starts to disperse. People congratulate the speakers; families begin to gather their members together. But Sean doesn't hang around . . . he has a baseball game to play.

THE ECHO

It is Memorial Day 1939. In the little southern Illinois town of Flora, the peonies are in bloom. The local florist does a brisk business in peonies among townsfolk who use them to trim the graves of loved ones.

For this day is still known as "Decoration Day," a time of remembrance that, according to the legend, began in the waning days of the Civil War when a few compassionate Southern women adorned the graves of both Union and Confederate soldiers buried near the battlefield where they fell. The official birthplace of Memorial Day, as recognized by the U.S. Congress in 1866, is Waterloo, New York. Two years later

General John A. Logan, an Illinois war hero, sponsored its designation as an official national holiday of remembrance.

In 1939, it is a day of solemn honor. There are no "Memorial Day Sale" banners on storefronts; businesses are closed; the streets are empty, except for those surrounding the city's small park, which is redolent with the pungent fragrance of lilacs. Flanked by the tan brick Methodist church and the gray stone Carnegie Library, the green square is packed with people.

The flag-bedecked wooden bandstand creaks under the weight of city fathers and American Legion men in natty blue uniforms with Sam Browne belts. The mayor talks about how "we remember our heroes who died so we can all be free." Other dignitaries speak while city band members, perspiring under the hot morning sun, stand ready with glinting brass instruments.

Several fragile ashen-faced Civil War veterans now in their nineties sit in the back of open touring cars beside the bandstand. Some slowly fan themselves with their wide-brimmed Grand Army of the Republic hats. Some doze. They've heard it many times before.

The speeches are finally over. As the speakers shuffle from the dais, the band members assemble for their march down Main Street to the Elmwood Cemetery on the west edge of town. The townspeople will follow in a slow procession of cars. One couple slips into their 1937 Oldsmobile. Already sitting in the backseat is their daughter, a high school sophomore. And nestled into the upholstery of the seat beside her is a silver trumpet.

The band starts the procession, playing "Stars and Stripes

Forever." The touring cars trail behind. The old men of the Grand Army of the Republic (the Civil War version of today's American Legion) stare resolutely ahead through cataract-fogged eyes. Are they thinking of Chickamauga? Antietam? Gettysburg? Boys on crepe paper–bedecked bicycles gleefully wheel in and out among the cars. Four of them will die at Pearl Harbor, two to be entombed forever in the battleship *Arizona*.

The band comes to parade rest at the quiet cemetery bordered by spring-leafed woods and the freshly turned loam of soybean fields. Cars park along the cemetery wall and people respectfully assemble around the monument dedicated to those who died in the Great War. The minister tugs at his collar, moist with perspiration, and picks up his black leather-bound Bible to give the invocation.

"Taps" sounds the end of the day's activities in Camp Kineowatha, Wilton, Maine, in 1940.

The girl leaves her parents' side and, hiding her trumpet under an arm, walks toward the rear of the cemetery. Late-morning dew beads her brown-and-white saddle shoes. A mourning dove calls from its perch high in an oak tree.

Looking over at the crowd to judge her distance, she stands

behind a moss-covered granite tombstone. A stone's throw away are her grandparents' worn markers. One day her parents will lie here.

She listens to the distant voices coming from the crowd and shivers, recalling what she'd heard the town's police chief say at her parents' dinner table the night before. He had been talking about his experiences as a young doughboy in Europe during the Great War, and the horror he and his fellow soldiers felt when, under furious fire from German troops, they watched the greenish-yellow clouds of poison gas waft toward their trenches. He vowed he'd kill himself before going "over there" again.

Someone recites "In Flanders' field, the poppies grow, between the crosses, row on row . . ."

Then it is time for the salute. Six Legionnaires raise Springfield rifles to the cerulean-blue sky and fire three volleys. The sharp explosions echo over the distant woods, startling a flock of crows that explodes from the trees complaining raucously.

A man from the band steps forward, stands still for a moment as if in prayer, raises a trumpet to his lips. The crowd is quiet. Some bow their heads, others place their right hand over their hearts, and the former military men snap sharp salutes.

The clear peal of "Taps" sounds over the cemetery, beyond the green soybean shoots, across the adjoining dusty road. A dusty pickup truck brakes to a halt as the driver recognizes the melody.

As the last note fades, the girl behind the tombstone

silently counts to ten, turns from the group at the monument to face the dark woods, raises her trumpet, and plays the echo.

There is something surreal about the distant notes drifting back to the crowd. They have an eerie quality, as if phantom lines of men, forever young, respond from eternity. *Remember . . . remember . . . remember.*

Eyes glisten, men and women wipe their cheeks, children stare at their shoes. All stand silent for a moment, lost in thought. Then they return to their cars and quietly drive away.

Back in the cemetery, a breeze ruffles the fresh-laid flowers as the girl tucks her silver trumpet under her arm and walks back to meet her waiting parents.

BIRTH OF THE ECHO

According to Jari A. Villanueva, master sergeant in the U.S. Air Force Band and noted authority on military music, "Taps" played with an accompanying echo "may have started right at the creation of the new call, when Union buglers played the tune for the first time at Harrison's Landing . . . Confederates across the James River repeated the new sound. . . . As the call grew in popularity it was not uncommon to hear the sound of "Taps" being performed at the same time each evening by buglers in other companies, thereby giving an echo effect."

Villanueva points out, however, that though sounding the echo is a popular element of Memorial Day services, it is not considered a proper part of the military service. For example, the playing of the echo is not permitted at Arlington National Cemetery, where "Taps" is sounded almost daily. (Interestingly, an "Echo Version" of "Taps" did appear in the *U.S. Marine Drum and Bugle Corps Manual* of 1959, but was dropped from later editions.)

Mike Spradlin of Lapeer, Michigan recalls the "magic" of hearing the echo while growing up in a small central Michigan farming town in the 1960s.

WHAT THE ECHO MEANS TO ME
BY MIKE SPRADLIN

My father, like nearly every adult male his age I knew, was a World War II veteran, which meant that our family's participation in Memorial Day festivities was mandatory. Every year, Dad marched in the parade as a member of the local VFW post color guard. Mom marched with the VFW Ladies' Auxiliary. Both of my older sisters marched with the high school band. As a small child, I decorated my bike with

Mike Spradlin in the second grade, around the time he joined the Cub Scouts.

red, white, and blue crepe paper and rode it in the parade. And when I was old enough, I marched in the parade as a member of the Cub Scouts.

My father's World War II service loomed large in our lives. As I approach middle age, I realize how fortunate I am; I've never had to fight in a war, as did my father and his comrades. Their shared experiences, both on and off the battlefield, bound them together in a way that I understand intellectually, but have never known on an emotional level. It is a bond that goes deeper than friendship, and has outlived even death.

Memorial Day was important to my dad. He had lost a brother at Normandy, and though he seldom spoke of his tour of duty, I'm sure he witnessed many things he would rather have forgotten. And during my youth, while the Vietnam War dragged on, and antiwar demonstrations raged around the country, my father would brook no talk of such dissent. We went to the parade. We saluted the flag. And we paid tribute to those who had made the ultimate sacrifice.

To this day I still remember my first Memorial Day parade as a Cub Scout. My enthusiasm for marching had convinced the den master that while I may have been too small and inexperienced to carry the pack's American flag, I should carry the troop flag. I recall putting on my uniform, just as I had seen my dad dress in his VFW uniform for so many years. We stood together in front of the hall mirror and inspected our uniforms before we left. He showed me how to straighten my belt and adjust my neckerchief so that it lay perfectly around my neck. It is one of the first memories I have of connecting with my father in that silent and unconscious way in which fathers pass certain knowledge along to their sons.

The Homer, Michigan, Memorial Day parade started at the east end of Main Street and we marched through our small downtown around the traffic circle. Ultimately, the marchers and onlookers gathered at the cemetery, a beautiful spot located on a wooded hillside just outside of town. There, a minister led us in prayer, asking God to hold close those men and women who had given their lives so that we might enjoy this day of remembrance in freedom. In my mind's eye, I can still see my father and the VFW color guard snap to attention, present arms, and fire the traditional twenty-one-gun salute. Even though at least twenty years had passed since they'd last seen active duty, their movements were as practiced and precise as those of the warriors they had once been. I scanned the solemn faces of those men until I found my father's, and wondered what thoughts were hidden behind his somber visage. Was he thinking of his brother? Or of the other men in his unit, with whom he had shared three years of his life? Did he wonder where they were now?

After the final rifle volley was fired, the color guard came to "parade rest," and a bugler stepped forward. The crowd had gone silent during the salute, and remained so as the notes of "Taps" rang out across the hillside. When the bugler finished he smartly returned the bugle to his side. That is when we heard it. *The echo*.

From down the hill, "Taps" sounded again. I'm

not sure how old I was before I realized that a second bugler, hidden in the woods at the bottom of the hill, sounded those notes. But to a small boy, standing at attention in the hot sun, it seemed like a real echo. And at the time I thought it was magic.

Memorial Day is no longer celebrated the way it was in the 1960s. My hometown no longer holds a Memorial Day parade. But, as in many towns across the country, there is a memorial in the center of town dedicated to residents who served their nation

Eighteen-year-old Hearl Spradlin, in 1943, the year he enlisted.

in the armed forces. A few years ago my mother purchased a brick to be placed in the walkway at the base of the monument. The brick bears my father's name. Not long ago I took my daughter Rachel, who never had a chance to meet her grandfather, to the monument to look for "Papa's Brick." After a few minutes of searching through the hundreds of names, we found it: Sergeant Hearl Spradlin, United States Army. We knelt there for a few moments tracing his name with our fingers. I answered her questions as best I could. She was then nearly the same age I was when I marched in my first Memorial Day parade.

Over the years I have heard "Taps" many times—from "lights out" at Scout camp when a scratchy recording played over the loudspeaker, to far too many funerals. Today, whenever "Taps" is played, I think of my father, of his sacrifice, and the sacrifices of so many other brave men. And I am instantly transported back to that cemetery outside my small hometown, listening again to the gentle sound of the notes echoing across the wooded hillside.

A MAN WHO HAS PLAYED "TAPS" MORE THAN 5,000 TIMES

Georgea Kovanis of the *Detroit Free Press* tells the fascinating story of volunteer bugler Dale Sprosty, who travels his state sounding "Taps" as his fellow veterans are laid to rest:

In a cemetery somewhere between the potato and bean fields that make up the mid-Michigan countryside, Dale Sprosty, seventy, wearing a dark overcoat, stood in the icy rain one afternoon last week and paid his respects to a soldier he didn't know.

He saluted, touching his right hand to the brim of his blue Army hat. He bowed his head for the chaplain's prayer. He watched intently as the Army representatives folded the American flag draped over the soldier's coffin and presented it to a grandson. He didn't flinch when the rifles fired.

Then, Sprosty raised his trumpet and started "Taps," the tune's mournful notes lingering in the air and then fading, slowly and gently like a memory.

This is what Sprosty, an Army veteran who lives in Broomfield Township just outside of Mt. Pleasant, does whenever and wherever he's called—setting off in his Ford Focus, sometimes with little notice and directions so incomplete he has to knock on the doors of farmhouses for help or flash his car's lights to flag down oncoming traffic, which is what he did on the way to the rainy cemetery service on Tuesday.

He's busier than ever, as the men and women who fought World War II are dying off in large numbers, doing about four funerals a week and sometimes two in one day. He figures the travel to funerals and memorials puts about thirty thousand miles a year on his car. He has played for five thousand services—including a local one for the people killed in the September 11 attacks—since 1948,

> I can honestly say that no matter where, when, or how I hear "Taps," I always break out in goose bumps, followed by tears.
>
> —*National Baseball Hall of Famer Phil Niekro*

when he began playing "Taps" at soldiers' funerals. He says he doesn't get nervous about performing, though his wife says that he seems more serious, more reserved on days he has a funeral and that she tries not to say much until he has completed his job.

On good days, Sprosty hits every note.

On not so good days, he misses some. And even though his sentiment is the same—he is thanking veterans of the armed forces one last time and making sure their survivors know the country appreciates their loved ones' service—he feels badly because "Taps" is the end.

And everyone hopes for a perfect ending.

Sprosty taught himself to play the trumpet when he was a kid and then he took lessons and got even better, playing as a teenager at joints in and around his hometown of Cleveland.

A year out of high school in 1948 and not so excited about his full-time job selling children's clothing at a May Company department store, Sprosty went along when a friend suggested they join the Army.

His first-choice assignment: to be a member of a military band.

Sprosty was dispatched to the prestigious First Army Concert Band, headquartered in New York City. The band played for funerals and in parades. It also surprised Gen. Dwight Eisenhower on his fifty-fifth birthday—something that still thrills Sprosty when he recounts the way Eisenhower shook each band member's hand and then sent two cases of ice-cold beer to the band's barracks.

On weekends, Sprosty often headed to Greenwich Village clubs with his trumpet and sat in with some of the greats—Tommy Dorsey, Artie Shaw, Harry James, Ray Anthony.

He married after joining the service and left the Army after four years, figuring the band's travel schedule would be too difficult on his young family. He moved back to Cleveland and went to work and continued to play at the funerals of friends and family members. Eventually divorced, he moved to Mt. Pleasant, where he was general manager of his uncle's bag manufacturing business, in nearby Edmore. He met his current wife, Christy Onstott, in 1989 when he dropped off clothes at the laundry service where she worked when she wasn't teaching preschool. She asked him out. He told her the relationship would never work because of their age difference—he's thirty-two years older. On their first date, he gave her an American flag pin. They've been married eleven years.

"You're patriotic and American from head to toe," Onstott said as Sprosty got ready for Tuesday's funeral.

Sprosty had continued to play "Taps" when he had time, but after he retired in 1993, he made it his full-time pursuit.

Otherwise, he says, "I'd be traveling or swimming in the ocean. There's nothing meaningful in doing that. We're not going to be on this earth forever. You may as well do something meaningful.

"That's what's wrong with the country. People are doing pleasure things and not doing anything for the good of the country."

He contacted veterans' organizations and funeral directors across the state, telling them he was available for services for honorably discharged veterans.

He doesn't charge a fee. ("By golly, I'm able to do it, so I'm doing it.") Every so often someone offers him a stipend and he turns it down. He pays his own travel expenses.

He doesn't like to schedule outings or social visits because he never knows when a funeral may come up, and the funerals are always his first responsibility. He knows there aren't enough trumpeters and he doesn't like the thought of a veteran being laid to rest with a taped recording. He's not sure it provides family members with the same sort of comfort—hearing the mournful tune allows a former soldier's loved ones to address their grief.

"If you were burying your husband or father, you would have tears," he says. "Your emotions are more released than if they were pent up. To hear "Taps" and know the respect the government has put to you, for you and your departed one, releases the sadness you have in your heart."

On Tuesday, in the cold rain, Sprosty missed a note.

Then he missed another and he shut his eyes and grimaced and wished he could play the whole thing over.

He didn't know the dead veteran's family. All he knew was the veteran's last name—Pollock.

As usual, he wondered if anyone had been comforted by the sound.

He hoped so.

But he drove away from the cemetery near Crystal not knowing that Mr. Pollock's brother—himself a veteran—felt himself standing a little taller and a little straighter when he heard the tune, pleased his brother was being honored and remembered.

There are caring, giving men like Dale Sprosty all over the nation who go out of their way to make sure that "Taps" is included in the final respects paid to their departed comrades.

Frank Calistro of Woodbridge, Connecticut, is a seventy-six-year-old World War II combat veteran who offers to sound "Taps" at the funerals of fellow military personnel in his immediate area. He considers this a duty as well as a privilege. A former trumpeter with the renowned Guy Lombardo Orchestra, he is wont to add a few bars of "America the Beautiful" or "God Bless America" to his musical offering.

And then there's the honor guard of the American Legion Mason-Dixon Post 194 in Rising Sun, Maryland, who show up—rain or shine—for an average of two funerals per week.

Krista Kelly McNeill of Johnson City, Illinois, was so moved by the men who honored her brother, Specialist Michael J. McNeill, that she hopes to join the military someday. "Off in the distance was heard a beautiful noise, rolling off the end of the young man's bugle," she wrote. "Each note slowly tearing away at me, making it easier to let go—each note bringing the remembrance of my brother and how he served his country, his family, his God."

Specialist Ronald Hedricks prepares to sound "Taps" during a ceremony in tribute to the late former president Dwight D. Eisenhower.

These are just a few examples of how the singular quality of "Taps" can bring out the best in us all.

Day Is Done

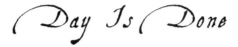

*O*n a Sunday afternoon when I was a teenager in Oak Park, Illinois, I was in my room preparing to go to a meeting at church. My little Montgomery Ward radio was tuned to WGN; a symphony was playing.

When I heard the announcer break in with "the Japanese have attacked Pearl Harbor," I knew in my heart that our world was changed forever.

As I stood at my office window in midtown Manhattan one morning nearly sixty years later, staring in disbelief at the horrible black banner of smoke roiling across the piercing blue sky, I knew that our world was utterly changed yet again.

Perhaps never in our country's history has "Taps" sounded more often than it did during the dark days following September 11, 2001.

In addition to the almost three thousand souls lost in the Twin Towers, hundreds of heroic firefighters, police officers, and rescue workers gave their lives that day rushing into burning buildings to pull victims to safety, heedless of their own danger. The courageous passengers of United Flight 93

A Marine bugler blows "Taps" at dedication services of First Marine Division cemetery in Okinawa, Japan, July 15, 1945.

sacrificed their lives as they rushed the hijackers, crashing their plane into the ground outside Pittsburgh rather than allowing it to complete its suicide attack on a more populated target. And terror struck at the very heart of our nation as the Pentagon, the seemingly impenetrable symbol of our nation's security, was ripped open and hundreds more innocent lives were claimed.

The aftermath was mind-numbing. So many funerals were being held, often on the same day, that New York mayor Rudy Giuliani pleaded for citizens to attend as many as they could, even if they did not know the deceased, to help console grief-stricken families and fellow survivors.

One police officer who attended more than thirty funerals

was asked what moved him the most. "Three things," he said with quiet emotion. "The casket carried on top of the slow-moving fire truck, the wail of the bagpipes, and the sound of 'Taps.' I have never known a song to be so healing. Whenever I hear that call, I give thanks for the men and women of the police and fire departments."

One New York Fire Department veteran, Tyrone Johnson, FDNY Engine 1, Ladder 24, was there in the midst of the holocaust. He says that the question he gets asked most is "How do you go on?" He responds by saying that when you become a firefighter, you aren't just going into a line of work, you're joining a family. And as in any family, you celebrate the good times together, and pitch in and help each other through the rough times. And, you honor your fallen brethren by remembering how they lived their lives helping others, and by carrying on doing the same, in their memory.

Family . . . human beings united in selfless endeavor for others. That has been personified by the American people in their outpouring of grief-stricken sympathy, in their gifts of blood, service, money, clothing, medical supplies, and so on. Men and women—from Fortune 500 executives to suburban "soccer moms," from all walks of life and all parts of the nation—have come together in the spirit of compassion to aid the victims of the September 11 attacks.

"In these times of national jeopardy, my heart wells up with tears of compassion and pride as I think of that haunting melody so tied to the ultimate sacrifice made by our brave and patriotic protectors."

—Actress Carol Lawrence

As I saw how my fellow Americans responded so courageously and resolutely to the attacks and terrorism that followed, I realized that just as we emerged from World War II a stronger and better nation, so would we survive—and triumph over—this new challenge. After World War II was ended, I was proud of how our country helped bring relief to enemy and

Firefighter Tyrone Johnson.

ally alike through our Marshall Plan and other programs. And I feel confident we will continue as a humanitarian people. For in the aftermath of the terrorists' attacks, I have been impressed by so many people coming together, regardless of religion, status, or nationality, yet bound by common humanity. I've seen abundant evidence of the true nature of faith and hope that unites us all in the face of hate.

Out of our common tragedy has emerged a new American family, one resolute in courage, selflessness, and compassion, people who from now on, whenever they hear the call of "Taps," will bow their heads and open their hearts in homage to the heroes of September 11, 2001.

Police officer Edward Harrigan plays "Taps" at the funeral of a fellow police officer in the wake of September 11, 2001.

I became an NYPD police officer in 1988 and have been the "Taps" player for the department since 1992. I've done hundreds of funerals for fallen cops, sergeants, and all the way up the chain of command.

With the recent events of September 11, I have been doing funerals for both cops *and* firemen (due to the fact the NYFD cannot handle the number of funerals on their own) every day. For the last month, the head "Taps" player for the NYFD and I have teamed up and made sure that every funeral—and that's almost four hundred so far—has been covered by a trumpeter/bugler. The numbers are staggering.

—*Edward Harrigan, police officer*

Acknowledgments

I am indebted to the following people for their help and support in the writing of *Taps:*

My wife, Betty, who put up with the twin distractions of my clattering typewriter and bugle calls at all hours;

My son Peter for his indefatigable research, knowledge, and counsel. Without him, there would be no book;

My son Kit for his sage advice on all things historical and military;

Jennifer Brehl, my editor and daughter-in-law, who made sure this book was written right—and on time;

My brothers Herb (a fellow WWII veteran) and Don (a veteran of WWII and the Korean War), who helped me remember;

Sharon Azar, my assistant, for her help and patience;

Jari A. Villanueva, master sergeant of the United States Air Force Band at Bolling Air Force Base, Washington, D.C. Jari is, most likely, the foremost expert on "Taps" in the world, and I am deeply grateful to him for sharing his extensive knowledge;

Michael Morrison, publisher of William Morrow, for seeing the worth in this book;

Mike Spradlin, manager of national accounts at William Morrow, whose memory enhanced it;

Betty Lew, who designed these pages so beautifully;

Barbara Levine, for the inspiring jacket design;

The "library ladies" in Rye, New York, for their gracious assistance;

Those who have shared with me their memories, thoughts, and feelings about "Taps"—your anecdotes have brought this book to life;

And, finally, to all the men and women who have served their country: my undying gratitude and respect.

For more information on the fascinating bugle call "Taps," consult the work of musicologist and military historian Jari A. Villanueva, master sergeant of the United States Air Force Band at Bolling Air Force Base in Washington, D.C. Master Sergeant Villanueva's fascinating and comprehensive fifty-page booklet on "Taps" and the music surrounding it is available through jvmusic@erols.com.

Text and Illustration Credits

Thanks to the following parties for permission to include excerpts from copyrighted sources:

The article "When day is done, Volunteer bugler Dale Sprosty travels Michigan blowing 'Taps' to lay veterans to rest," by Georgea Kovanis, originally published October 22, 2001, in the *Detroit Free Press,* is reprinted by permission of the *Detroit Free Press.*

Excerpt from Tyrone Johnson is from "Out of the Ashes." Reprinted with permission from *Guideposts* magazine. Copyright © 2001 by Guideposts, Carmel, NY 10512. All rights reserved.

Excerpts from *Twenty-Four Notes That Tap Deep Emotions* by Jari A. Villanueva are reprinted by permission of the author.

Excerpt from *Taps* by Willie Morris. Copyright © 2001 by Joanne Prichard Morris and David Rae Morris. Reprinted by permission of Houghton Mifflin Company. All rights reserved.

The poem "Taps," from *Ghosts and Echoes* by Ann Cragg, copyright © 1999 by Ann Cragg, is reprinted by permission of the author.

The poem "Freedom Is Not Free" by Kelly Strong, copyright © 1981 by Kelly Strong, is reprinted by permission of the author.

Illustrations: page x, photograph copyright Robert Capa/Magnum Photos; page 3, courtesy of Richard H. Schneider; page 7, painting by Sidney King, courtesy of Berkeley Plantation, Charles City, Va.; page 9, painting by William M. Hunt, photograph courtesy of Davison Art Center, Wesleyan University; page 10, etching by Edwin Forbes; page 12, painting by Sidney King, courtesy of Berkeley Plantation; page 18, courtesy of United States Army Quartermaster Corps; page 25, photograph by Alexander Gardner, courtesy of the National Archives (Brady Collection); page 26, photograph copyright by Underwood & Underwood/CORBIS; page 28, courtesy of Herschel C. Logan; page 33, photograph by Matthew Brady, courtesy of the National Archives (Brady Collection); page 37, courtesy of Josef A. Orosz Jr.; page 39, courtesy of Jari Villanueva; page 45, courtesy of the National Archives (photo #042244); page 49, drawing courtesy of the British Museum; page 51, photograph copyright Michael Freeman/CORBIS; page 56, photograph copyright CORBIS; page 61, courtesy of Berkeley Plantation; page 62, courtesy of Berkeley Plantation; page 64, courtesy of the Chapel of the Centurion, Fort Monroe, Va.; page 65, courtesy of Public Affairs Office, U.S. Army Military District of Washington; page 67, courtesy of Sandra Harris; page 73, courtesy of Paul Haring, U.S. Army; page 76, courtesy of U.S. Army; page 81, courtesy of Public Affairs Office, U.S. Army Military District of Washington; page 83, courtesy of Jari Villanueva; page 84, image courtesy of Jari Villanueva; page 89, image courtesy of Josef A. Orosz Jr.; page 93, photograph copyright Hulton-Deutsch Collection/CORBIS; page 98, courtesy of Al Michael Cioffi; page 102, courtesy of Ann Cragg; page 108, photograph copyright Bettmann/CORBIS; page 115, courtesy of Michael Spradlin; page 118, courtesy of Michael Spradlin; page 125, courtesy of the National Archives (photo #SC650066); page 127, courtesy of the National Archives (photo #127GW-612); page 129; photograph copyright by John Blais; page 130, photograph copyright Ed Betz.